William B. Foreignerski, as his name suggests, is a foreigner. He came to the UK to find work, earn a pound and then leave. Instead, he learned the local language and stayed, charmed by the country and its people.

Is he a gain for the economy? Read the book and decide yourself.

To all my brothers and sisters in the construction trade.

William B. Foreignerski

STROIKA WITH A LONDON VIEW

AUSTIN MACAULEY PUBLISHERS™

LONDON • CAMBRIDGE • NEW YORK • SHARJAH

A CIP catalogue record for this title is available from the British Library.

ISBN 9781788485289 (Paperback)
ISBN 9781788485296 (Kindle e-book)
ISBN 9781528954525 (ePub e-book)

www.austinmacauley.com

First Published (2019)
Austin Macauley Publishers Ltd
25 Canada Square
Canary Wharf
London
E14 5LQ

Without Jan Kijowski, I would have never learnt to use a cordless drill properly. Without Paul Valentine, I would have never learnt to write in English. Thank you, gentlemen!

Chapter 1

The Millennium crashed down upon me to the accompaniment of yelling twin babies, an absolute lack of money and uncertain hopes in the musical field. How was it that others had it all, and I didn't? There had always been stupid songs on the radio, and it seemed bloody obvious to me that anybody could write shit like that. Catchy chorus, sappy lyrics, and money should just pour into your bank account like a mountain stream. But no, it hadn't worked that way for me.

What with having to borrow money for nappies for the third time; life was pissing me off terribly, and my utter unemployability in the Latvian job market was suffocating me. Every day, there were the same job adverts in the newspapers, clear evidence that in Eastern Europe the only way to make business was by exploiting retards of proletarian persuasion – either by charging an agency fee and not providing a job or by offering lots of hard work for remuneration insufficient even to keep their landlords happy. I could only marvel at the uniformity of the ads. It seemed that the brains that created them were not bright enough to come up with new ideas to catch the same people twice.

Song after song of mine had been rejected by the stations or never made it into the charts. My girlfriend, who had fallen in love with me because I was an aspiring rock star on the rise, now complained about me going to rehearsals and spending time in the studio. The kids were growing, and my mother-in-law, who reluctantly provided accommodation for us, hated me more and more.

Then, Shane McGowan visited Riga, our capital city. I hadn't the money to go to the gig but luckily had met an ex-classmate with loads of cash who was happy to buy me a drink or two at an old-time Irish pub nearby. We were sitting there chatting, when Shane's bodyguards stormed in to scout the terrain after the gig was over. A moment later, the legend himself appeared – drunk out of his mind and held up on both sides by members of his crew. We asked for permission to snap a photo with him, and it was generously granted. The limp arms of the semi-comatose artist went round our shoulders; he instinctively revealed his dental remains to the camera in an imitation of a smile, and – click! Either the concert or the booze, or both, had robbed Shane of the ability to communicate, so instead of fan talk, we simply retreated to our table.

When I think about it now, it appears an event that was to have a profound and magical impact on what happened later.

Armand, the ex-classmate with the cash I mentioned before; whom I had met totally unexpectedly earlier that day, added a couple of beers to the wide array of glasses already on Shane's table and then re-joined me. He had just returned from England and had lots of cash on him. He looked at me, I thought, with ill-concealed pity. Unlike me, he called glasses of beer 'pints', which sounded bizarre to my ears. Where I'm from, we deal with litres, not pints.

"You must go to London," Armand told me. "Hundred quid a day in construction work, and for the most part, you have to do nothing. When I first went, I didn't know how to bang a nail in a wall. All you have to do is simply get your ass out there and be active. I can lend you some money to start with, if you like. You can return it when you've settled down properly."

I stared at him in surprise, trying to digest the idea.

"Do you think I could earn some decent cash within a few months?"

"Yep. Any *stroika*[1] will be a quick fix for that. It all depends on how lucky you are and how quickly you are able to adapt to

---

[1] The Russian-English dictionary says that *стройка* means 'building site'. But wait, it also means other things. It defines how you dress on and off work. It means back pain, from thoracic and lumbar all the way down to sacral. It encompasses a huge vocabulary of everyday interaction. It means builder's tea and builder's bum, it means the smell of cut metal and wet cement added to your sweat, it means your way of life and your life's ways. All that and even more, as we shall see.

their way of doing things over there, to accommodate yourself to their various employment schemes. Easy."

'Easy' was an appealing expression and 'schemes', was a word with profound meaning. They were both... fascinating. Their sound possessed a melodic charm, like a white witch's spell. They had a ring to them, almost an exotic accent hinting at a faraway land where it rains wine and where streets are paved with gold. In the brave new world into which the great vacuum cleaner of life was about to suck me, accommodating to 'schemes' meant finding food, getting a roof over your head, earning cash and obtaining everything else that Prof Maslow has identified in his hierarchy of needs. The famous pyramid, you know. Sleep and food at the bottom, self-realisation at the top.

At the time, I didn't have a clue. I simply sipped some beer, wiped the foam off and waited for the brain cells to rearrange themselves in new, yet unfamiliar networks.

Meanwhile, a bunch of tipsy women in the grip of their midlife crisis had swarmed around McGowan, knocking on the doors of his consciousness with chatter in Latvianised pidgin. The bartender put 'The Summer in Siam' on. Poor groupies, they looked to me, all wanting a piece of their bygone youth back, even if that piece was worn out and didn't smell too good. Admittedly, Shane tried his best to moan something in response but his fingers were constantly stroking the table, obviously in the hope of coming into contact with a comforting cold glass. A freckled bodyguard wedged his massive beer gut between the legend and a particularly overt admirer. *If I ever succeeded in my musical ambitions, would this become my future, too?*

I chased the thought away and focused instead on the main fantasy of mine at the time – a laptop with a whole lot of music software on it. I'd never had a laptop of my own and I was fed up with chasing after the lucky sods who happened to have a computer and trying to organise a recording session. As a band, we couldn't afford a proper studio too often, and that drove me mad. If I had my own mini studio, I would enjoy inviting people to come along and play, rather than begging to be allowed in their studios. I'd get rid of my debts, have happy children for whom I could buy all the presents they wanted, and above all, have the ability to continue the struggle standing up, rather than being pressed down to the ground.

In other words, I had been drowning for too long. What I was longing for was to stick my head out of the water.

I pondered what Armand had told me. *A hundred pounds a day, eh?* If I worked twenty days a month, it came to a total of…that's right, two-thousand. In Latvia, two-hundred a month was considered not too bad. And it went without saying that I was ready, willing and able to work not only Saturday and Sunday but day and night as well. Of course, I had thought about the idea of a short-term economic immigration before – I had even asked around. There were a few ambitious guys who had promised a job in England or Ireland on the condition that I got past the immigration officers on my own. The immigration people interviewed everyone who intended to cross the border. It sounded like a scary thing to go through. On top of that, I had heard some terrible stories about stolen passports and people being sold into slavery and forced to work in brothels.

At least Armand was a person I trusted.

Meanwhile, Shane had exhausted the last of his energy and was being steered towards the loo before leaving. Back in 2000, British tourists did not bet with each other to have a piss on the Freedom Monument in the centre of Riga, as they do now. I doubt they remember Mathias Rust and the ideals he stood for. In 1987, Rust landed on Moscow's Red Square in a Cessna 172 light aircraft, claiming it as an act of goodwill to minimise tensions between East and West and to prove Russian border defence to be rubbish. Well, a lot of time has passed since Rust risked his challenge to the Soviet military. Today, things have changed. People are far less political. Today, folks rarely think beyond having stag nights in countries where the majority of the female population are genetically blonde and beer is cheap, and make bets on their skill to fool the police and piss on national monuments.

So Shane McGowan went for a leak in the gents, as you would expect any respectful guest in your country to do, even if they can barely stand.

We also left and emerged into the humid darkness, which was adorned with dotted lights threading the streets towards the nearby Old Town plaza. A nervous pigeon was pacing in the light of the pub's entrance, its red eye expressing discomfort and complete lack of comprehension of what the hell he was doing there at that time of night. I inhaled the chilly mist of Old Riga and held my breath for a moment. I had made my decision. There was nothing to lose anyway; at worst, I would only end up deeper in debt. But you know what? Once you're deep in shit, to stay there a little longer does not appear to be such an awful thing anymore. You can get used to anything. On the other hand, the opportunity to escape was worth its weight in gold. I had drunk a lot of beer, but it wasn't only the alcohol. The golden river of lager now mixed with adrenalin, whatever colour that is, and the sky above the tiny circle lit by the street lamps exploded in mysterious promises. I was being lured to step outside immediate, well-known territory, which after all was only a grey pavement covered with a slick film of mud. The sky above was invisible beyond the glow of the streetlights, yet I knew it was full of stars. Like all city dwellers, unconsciously I longed to see the Milky Way every night.

Somebody touched my shoulder. I stepped aside and Shane McGowan went past me, head hung low, supported by the arms of the two massive chaps escorting him. Somewhere nearby there would be a car waiting to transport him away from our circle of light on a grey Riga pavement.

We hid our hands in our pockets for warmth and also headed for our car, but in the opposite direction.

***

The night before I left, I sat by the open stove in the bedroom of our little flat, together with the twins and their mom. The soft, sleepy silence of the suburbs outside was interrupted every hour by the squeaky noise of the night tram as it took the bend round the graveyard on the opposite side of the street. The window sill and the bird feeder outside were wrapped in snow, and cold radiated from the window. The smoke of my cigarette got caught in the flow of air and escaped behind the curtain of flames inside the open stove mouth. We were not allowed to smoke in the kitchen, as that would offend and annoy grandma. She was constantly pissed off anyway, but what the heck, I figured I might as well leave without another bust-up.

So there we sat, sharing a fag in awkward silence with our heads together, close to the stove opening. Actually, smoking had become just about the only thing we did together anymore. Goodbye sex? Nothing of that kind had happened between us for quite a while. I considered it to be a consequence of our money worries as well as our general weariness with life.

"I'll try to send you some money as soon as I can."

"Yeah, see what you can do. I'm paying for the nursery at the end of the next week. Firewood should last for about a couple more months."

In that part of the town, stove heating was still the norm. It had seemed so romantic once, with the orange blaze crackling, hissing and sending sparks rushing up the flue. Occasionally, the grey smoke of my Marlboro seeped slowly towards the stove's mouth and then slipped into the cracks around the door frame, without even making it to the opening itself. The previous summer I had thought of buying some asbestos cord to block the cracks before the winter started, but somehow I had always turned out to be too busy with something else.

And then Armand sounded his horn outside, and I left.

There were three of us on the road; Armand's wife was trying to help a friend of hers the same way Armand was trying to help me. The wife's friend was an aristocratic-looking, slim stunner with the old-fashioned name Lillian. We squeezed ourselves into the tiny sports car. There wasn't much space there, so it was a good thing I had chosen to take only a sleeping bag and a guitar.

The car ran through the outskirts of Riga, past Jurmala, and on towards Liepaja, where we were supposed to take a ferry across to Germany. Anybody with a brain tries to avoid the vast expanse of Poland, especially in wintertime. Family, friends and ambitions were all left behind. My musical projects were to go into hibernation until spring. I remembered saying goodbye to my son, shaking his tiny hand (a gesture he did not yet understand) and hugging my daughter. I could still picture the flames in the bedroom stove, but now the actual heat was emanating from the vents in the dashboard of the car. We turned Metallica all the way up and sat back. Oh, Land of Milk and Honey, here we come!

The ferry was big and bright with halogen lighting, giving as much light as was possible to get in the middle of the grey and wintery Baltic Sea. We had to spend some twenty-four hours on the ferry and ended up drinking by default. Lillian's phone rang almost non-stop with relatives wanting to know every detail of her progress, but the power of telephone control card ended once we hit open waters, thank goodness.

People on the road meet each other much more quickly and easily than in other circumstances. When the effect of the alcohol is enhanced by the naturally swaying surroundings, conversations quickly become more open-minded and friendly. At the bar, we got unexpectedly acquainted with a stranger called Pete, who was gulping down shots of Stolichnaya one after another and joined us in the conversation right away, without any ceremonial excuse. The guy was in his fifties, had a bald patch on the top of the head, and a face completely red from alcohol. He had lots of opinions and emotions to share, too.

"Four years now I've been living in Germany," he explained to me. "Four fucking years. In the beginning, I did some farm work, but there wasn't any decent money in it. I never managed to learn the language, and the first year was especially tough. Now I am working for a Jewish guy from Ukraine, delivering goods for his shop. Whole of my life I've been working as a driver. Shite, I'm a Liepaja[2] boy! We last long. He keeps me in the job because I work at least ten hours a day and seven days a week. Now I have just had my first vacation in three years. Mate, I have fucked up everything – my wife left me, and my daughter doesn't talk to me anymore. I bought her a pair of earrings… expensive ones. She threw them into the rubbish bin. All because of money."

His large, brutish worker's hands clenched into fists and the sparse grey hair on his thick fingers stuck out white against his scarlet skin. He definitely was a Liepaja boy – you could tell it from his Western Latvian accent, especially when he apologised and left to 'bomit'. Upon his return, Pete immediately knocked back another shot[3] then straightened and squinted at me.

_____

[2] A harbour town in western Latvia, famous for its distinctive accent.

[3] I think I should explain the Latvian idea of a 'shot'. It is not the ridiculous fly's piss amount they drop in your shot glass in British bars and pubs (that is, twenty-five grams). For east Europeans, a shot is traditionally one-hundred grams, although recently under EU legislative pressure they have unfortunately been dished out in

"Which way are you heading?"

Through Germany to England, we told him. Pete threw his hands up in the air. England is a difficult one to get into, he explained (and at the time it really was). It wasn't worth the risk, even though you could earn more money there than anywhere else in Europe. Pete was also apprehensive about the British immigration officers because not only could they screw you, throw in gaol and then deport you from the country at the expense of the queen. They could also blacklist you, and then getting around Europe became much more difficult. To enter England through the front door wasn't a good idea, he said. In France, however, there were some Lithuanians who could get you across the English Channel in fishermen's boats. You hid in the boat among the cod and herring, and they let you out somewhere in the Southampton area. Personally, Pete would do it that way; it was safer and wiser. His cousin and her daughter were living and working in France, in a meat factory. They'd earned enough for a big house in Latvia, near the village of Virgas, and a brand new Mazda.

"They've kept the car in beautiful condition, untouched like a nude sculpture in a museum. They drove it home straight from the shop and have kept in the garage ever since. It's only been on the road a couple of times, so that nothing bad can happen to their precious. They are never at home to drive it anyway. They live in France most of the time. They work so hard. When I look at the hands of those women, you know..."

Pete stared for a second at his own massive paws, all scratched and rough as gardener's spades, and then held them up for my inspection.

"Horrible. My cousin's skin is all split up, and she's suffering from arthritis already. She works so much... Did I tell you: the main thing is to find the right Lithuanians to take you across La Manche to England? After that, you must find an Eastern European colony[4], and then – that's it."

---

smaller and smaller units, even in Latvia.

[4] You might call them 'diasporas' or 'minority ethnic groups', or 'communities', but we ourselves say 'colonies'. After all, they are in exotic lands far, far away, where exotic and bizarre creatures roam and exotic and bizarre humans do weird things. And we do

"What do you mean – that's it?" I asked.

"That's it means that's it! You don't need anything else. They will know what to do. They will find you a job, and you won't have any problems with the language. Mate, I'm totally fine with the Russian lingo anywhere in the world because all our folks – well, our ex-folks, from the Soviet-influenced territories – you know what I mean – they all speak Russian. Lithuanians, Ukrainians... never deal with the Poles, though. They're cunts. They steal our jobs, working for even less money than we do. If you need any documents – indeed, anything, for fuck's sake, find yourself a Lithuanian, he'll do anything for you. For the money, that is. But don't let him fuck you over. Be vigilant, you know what I mean? As for the locals, they are just plain assholes. I bet you think the English, the French, the Germans are nice, normal people just like us, don't you? Bollocks. You know why? Because we never actually knew any of them in the wild, as it were, and our understanding about those bloody foreign capitalist cunts came from Soviet films, where foreign characters were played by our own actors. That's why you think they must be normal people. But they have nothing inside! No soul, just money. They are empties, not humans – that's what westerners are. Simply rich bastards, that's all. You can't even have a proper conversation with them, they're such assholes. I've been suffering from them for four fucking years now. I know what I'm saying."

"You said you don't speak German."

"I can tell an asshole straightaway when I see one. Has a wife and two kids, works in a bank, drives a brand new car... nothing but pigs, every single one of them."

He gulped down another shot then chased it with a gherkin for *zakuska*[5] and continued.

"But above all, be careful with Latvians. No one is going to fuck a Latvian over so unashamedly and painfully as another

---

send the raw resources (i.e. money) back to the metropolitan state.

[5] There are secrets to good vodka drinking. I'll share some with you: first, drink it from the freezer. The less you feel the taste, the better. Second, eat something right after–best, a gherkin, or a slice of smoked ham, or something like that. We call this *zakuska*. With vodka, it's how you drink it that makes it not only effective, but also enjoyable.

Latvian. I used to have a friend, who lives in Berlin. *Used* to have. When I arrived in the country I had nothing at all – and can you imagine what that cunt told me? I suffered when I first came here, he says, so now it is your turn to suffer. I won't give you a penny for support. Once you've settled, he says, gimme a ring and we'll talk then. Do you think I rang him even once? Hell no."

We sat silently for a while. Pete covered his face with one hand, the shot glass with a ferry sticker completely hidden in the other, and gave a quiet yet emotional hiccup. He then lowered his hand to stroke his beard, tears shining in his tired red eyes. I could feel waves of emotions washing over him.

By now, I had had too much myself, so I laid myself down on a seat by the fruit machines and tried to sleep. Every time the ferry woke me with its movement, I saw Pete still at the same spot, his head hanging down, exposing the red surface of the bald patch surrounded by grey hair. Half of a sandwich slid around the table between his glass and the bottle, back and forth. I wondered how much he had paid for a whole bottle at the bar, instead of wasting time with single shots like the rest of us had to. *So you can earn decent money, after all*, I thought to myself, shaping my hoodie into a pillow. During the night, I kept waking up as my pillow slid along the slippery seat, and every time I noticed that the bottle had been replaced by a new one, just as empty, even though Pete himself seemed to be as lonesome and motionless as before.

When we reached Lubeck, I was woken by the rush of passengers and a shrill voice speaking over the speakers. Pete lay under the table, completely stiff and with his arms wide apart as if he wanted to hug the whole floor of the ferry canteen. The redness had left his skull. From where I stood, his bald patch seemed as pale and grey as the remnants of hair around it. Everybody had to wait half an hour before getting off the ferry because we had to wait for the paramedics to take him off first.

As we disembarked, I asked the captain what had happened.

"*Nichts besonderes.*[6] He simply drank twice as much vodka as I have ever had in my whole life. Most people would have died if they were him. We just had a call from the hospital about his luggage. They've rinsed his stomach, and he's fine."

---

[6] Nothing special. *(German)*

Being from Riga, I suspected it must have been that special Liepaja upbringing that had saved him.

Chapter 2

Slim and elegant, in a grey jacket and black bowtie, Vasily Livanov opened a drawer and ran his fingers through a bunch of cards bearing the names of different criminals.

Ever since I was young I have marvelled, together with 250 million other people, at the exploits of Vasily Livanov because he was the one and only Sherlock Holmes we had in USSR. And we would all swear that he is still the best of them all.

Livanov then turned his head towards Vitaly Solomin (the no less spectacular Russian Dr Watson).

'Мэтьюз. Ну это тот самый, который выбил мне левый клык на Черинг-кросском вокзале.[7]'

Livanov fished a few cards out of the drawer and sat down, back straight, in a huge chair next to a beautifully decorated wooden table. His posture was noble and dignified, as one might expect of a true Victorian gentleman.

'Да, Ватсон, все это тени прошлого, которые могут ожить только с помощью вашего пера.[8]'

And he smiled like an angel, browsing through the cards again.

Wow, and here I stood, at the very same Charing Cross Station, staring in amazement at a map of London Underground. In the Russian movie, Sherlock Holmes knew every part of London by heart. He could tell which area of London you came

---

[7]'Matthews. The same chap who broke my left canine at Charing Cross Station.' *(Russian)*

[8] 'Yes, Watson, all these are shadows of the past which can come back to life only with the help of your pen.' *(Russian)*

from by the mud on your shoes; he knew where to buy cocaine; and he knew where that smartass Colonel Moran was hiding. The only criminal Conan Doyle never let Sherlock go after was Jack the Ripper, who was murdering prostitutes in the area known by the misleadingly innocent name of Whitechapel. Perhaps Sir Arthur had too much respect for the royal family – after all, it has been speculated that the maniac was one of them.

First time in London! I wish I could say of my first visit: There was fog everywhere. There was fog up and down the river, rolling defiled among the tiers of shipping, and the waterside pollutions of a great (and dirty) city, with people peeping over the parapets of Westminster Bridge into a nether sky of fog, with fog all around them, like they were standing in a hot-air balloon hanging in a clouded sky... but no. London was less Dickensian than I had expected. It was surprisingly warm and humid if judged by the standards of a Latvian winter. The birds were chirping like crazy and the buildings around me were veiled in a thin, milky mist of the sort you would rather expect above a waterfall in a rainforest, where the last of the dinosaurs survived.

We were all in a dazed state after the nerve-wrenching wait before the border and the rush of excitement after crossing it. On the M25, the big London orbital, exhaustion hit us like a ton of bricks. The ferry journey across the Channel has escaped my memory completely – we boarded, collapsed on the floor and came back to life only when it was the time to go downstairs to the car.

Lillian was still asleep on the back seat of the car, pale and fragile, and holding my guitar in her embrace as we headed into central London. When we reached Charing Cross, we ignored the parking restrictions and got out of the car for a moment or two to get some fresh air. I looked where the Strand disappeared into the mist in one direction and next saw a red double-decker diving into the same mist in the opposite direction. A lonesome ray of the sun made it through and lit the window of an old-fashioned tea shop across from the rail station. A Jamaican guy with dreads and a giant rasta cap passed us by and smiled a smile so big you would never be able to squeeze its equal out of any person in Latvia, not without plastic surgery anyway. Even though I didn't realise it then, the essence of London had begun to work quietly on me, soaking up through my body and soul.

"Will, get back in the car," Armand said nervously as a traffic policeman came towards us. "We're going to Dulwich."

I jumped back into my seat, so heavily the car swayed alarmingly. I bet the tiny vehicle was tired too after rolling such a long way over often poor and winding roads. We circled Trafalgar Square and the monument to England's one-eyed admiral. The lions seemed to be rather massive that morning, maybe because I was seeing them for the first time in my life.

I was glad we didn't stay in Dulwich for long. We started off by sharing a flat with a young man named Nansen and a young Irishwoman, who was an English teacher. If we ever had any contact with her, it was because she would be complaining about something. Mercifully, much of her time was spent either working or travelling to exotic destinations.

I wonder... *how many teachers from exotic destinations can afford to travel at all?*

To cut a long story short, the teacher was a bitch while Nansen was a friend and ex-classmate. Nansen had long black hair, a little goatee and elastic jeans that made his legs look as if he hadn't eaten for months. He loved blues and classic rock, and sometimes people called him Jesus for his looks. Nansen had been in London for quite a while, borrowing money off everyone because there was no work available. Christmas was coming and the British construction industry was getting ready for its winter hibernation. Lillian and I also borrowed lots of cash from local Latvian friends who had work at the time, and then we all held endless meetings over bottles of Vladivar, smoking rollups and discussing how easy and profitable work in London could be.

"All in all, the main thing is to relax and be friendly. Easy," Armand told us, watching out for the plastic cups we had all over the floor as he made his way back from the loo. We had nicked the cups from the nearby fish and chips eatery because we couldn't afford to buy any cutlery or kitchen ware.

"The English like it friendly," he continued. "Once I built a brick wall for an Englishman. I didn't know then that builders use spirit levels. While I was working, all seemed fine. But as soon as I finished and took a step back, wow! – The whole thing was a massive cock-up. Absolutely horrendous! I mean, almost every brick was at a different level and different angle because I didn't realise you should spread the muck evenly, but slapped it on each brick in a separate thickness. It was a complete piece of shit."

"Did he sack you?" Lillian asked, blowing out a puff of smoke.

"No way! He was over the moon with it. I shit you not! He was only paying me forty quid anyway. A proper English bricklayer would have asked at least half a grand, easy. Even though I had messed around on that wall for a whole two days, the guy had saved a lot of money using me. Later, he recommended me to the guy I am working for now."

We bit our tongues and resisted the temptation to ask if Armand's employer might have a job for us, too. We knew very well that there was nothing at the moment, anyway. It was in Armand's own interests to get us some source of income – we all owed him enough money to buy a decent second-hand car each. The sums were growing, even though he never charged us any interest. It was simply the fact that we were constantly calling on him to borrow something, almost every second day because everything cost us much more than we had expected.

And then even he ran out of money. He didn't have any job himself for a while, and the modest waitress income of his wife barely covered the family expenses they had themselves. We milked the last available money from their credit cards, rolled up the last of the Drum tobacco, then sat down opposite each other at the dirty kitchen table and had a smoke. The situation was definitely having a bad impact on us. Our nerves had been strung far too tight for far too long. Outside the window, the identical roofs of Dulwich's houses stretched in long rows like a never-ending clone army. Sometimes we were entertained by squirrels making themselves busy here and there, but I felt shitty nevertheless.

Before we were able to say anything constructive – which was especially difficult because everything had already been said a billion times anyway – in came the teacher, freshly returned from some Pacific island, to start complaining about us smoking in the kitchen. Nansen and I looked at each other and immediately made at least one decision – we had to move to a new place. That at least gave us a sense of direction. We kept the cigarette butts, to have something for later, and called Armand to let him know that we needed a new home, and quick. And we had no idea how to get it.

As always, Armand was able to sort it all out for us. Through her friends, his wife put us in touch with a bunch of Ukrainians, who were looking for somebody to share a house with. The Ukrainians did not know her, but she knew somebody who knew them. There used to be five Ukrainians living in the place, then one left. If he could be replaced by three Latvians moving in, the pressure on the only lavatory increased while pressure of rental expenses decreased, a deal that made Ukrainians happy. It was a typical immigrants' trade-off.

Two of them were brothers – Misha and Grisha, funny as that might sound. Then there were their friends Loha and Vlad. Loha worked in security and was almost never at home, while Vlad was almost never at home either because he worked as a kitchen porter. Even though the guys were from the Ukrainian city Vinnytsa, they knew almost no Ukrainian and even spoke Russian among themselves. Yet their Ukrainian patriotism was high, demonstrated every night in tea- and alcohol-soaked living room discussions.

As if by magic we had changed our environment from Dulwich to Leyton, right next to Stratford, where there is the highest concentration of Lithuanians and Pakistanis outside Lithuania and Pakistan, respectively. In our case, there was a big advantage in having Lithuanians around – there was a food shop, where we could buy Latvian snacks and black rye bread, and also *Restoranas Smilte,* a Lithuanian restaurant, where they served some Eastern European food. Our *braliukaslietuviškas*[9], as usual throughout history, were much smarter and quicker to settle down and make a profit. They were opening shop after shop, while the Latvians were still considering the pros and cons.

The house was built in a typical English yellow-brick style, it had two floors and a silly brick wall at the front (yeah, I challenge you to justify a wall you can simply step over – where I'm from, walls are for keeping people out, not an architectural adornment). Behind the house, there was a little garden, with a crooked apple tree in the centre and a rubbish heap in one corner.

---

[9] Lithuanian brothers. *(Lithuanian)*

Under the tree, we would later make our barbecues in a self-made *mangal*[10], smoke or simply sit around if it wasn't raining.

The landlord was an Indian, and never in my life have I seen a happier man. His smile never disappeared from his face, and he never forgot to mention what a lovely and great day it was today. Eastern Europeans call Indians Babay, or Babaychik, which means little Babay[11]. Many Indians actually like the sound of the word and teasingly apply it to the Eastern Europeans themselves. Each time he saw us, Jasvinder would make a happy 'hum hum' sound, giggle, then wave his hand with clattering golden bracelets and shout in a high-pitched voice:

"Babaychik! Hey, Babaychik! How are you today, boss?"

In Leyton, I began my agency era. First, you call an agency to register, then you fax them a copy of your documents and the details of the bank account you are going to use for your salary. Sounds simple, but we were not a part of the EU in those days and were required to have a business visa in our passports to work legally.

So I busied myself with cutting up photocopies of mine and Armand's passports and gluing them together, then making another photocopy of the glued version. You see, in his passport he had the key to unlock every building site in the country – a real business visa! The most difficult thing was to combine my passport photograph with his passport page because in Latvian passports, you had these three stars on top of the photograph. In some cases, these are more to the right, in some more to the left, but at the end of the day, I managed to do a pretty good job.

You might ask – if it is so simple, why didn't I simply send a photocopy of his passport in and pretend to be him. Well, you had to be careful. Armand didn't want to have too many people working in his name. He already had two friends pretending to be him – and they had been doing it long before us lot came along. He said he was happy with the amount of turnover on his account and the amount of the tax paid because it helped him to get the loans and mortgages he wanted, but too much would be suspicious. Oh, and the bank account for me and Nansen was the

---

[10] Grill.

[11] In Asian cultures, Baba is an honorific term meaning 'father', 'wise man', or 'sir'.

same; it was actually Liva's. We told the agencies that she was our girlfriend. Armand, accordingly, was presented as Lillian's boyfriend, so she could also receive her salary in a bank account. And so I faxed the combined passport photocopies from our local internet café and sat waiting for my big moment.

Some people don't like immigrants, but there are a few good things about us, you know. We happily work for peanuts, any time of day or night, without making any demands on social support or health care, and we don't give a damn about trade unions. We help our employers' expenses go down and income go up. A boss of a building company quite often demands from the customer the same, or nearly the same, sum he would ask if he had workers who understood and cared about their rights. However, he pays his immigrant workers about a half or even a third of the normal salary. The customers are happy – the immigrant workers work not only week days, but also evenings, weekends, and if necessary, during the night.

Capitalism is based upon expansion or, as I prefer to call it, the 'bicycle principle'. As long as you move forward, everything is fine and the money rolls in. But as soon as the cyclist stops, he falls off. That's why the swarms of hungry immigrants are not only the curse of the local proletarians but also the blessing for the local rich. Back in the day, quite interestingly, if you were an illegal immigrant and you happened to work for a local firm, the authorities could kick you out of the country at the expense of the queen and the taxpayer, but the employer had almost no responsibilities – at least not big enough to stop him hiring other cheap illegal labourers.

So the immigrant is happy about the money, the boss about the profit and the customer about the amount of work done. Is there anybody at all who might be unhappy with this arrangement? I'm afraid so. Those are the local folks, the simple workers who find it harder to pay their bills because of us.

Meanwhile, the New Year was upon us. The Ukrainians, who were a very friendly and bubbly bunch, kept paying for the alcohol because they had had work right up to Christmas Day itself. Our rent was paid by Armand, as usual. The only problem was starvation – and I mean that quite literally. There were too many of us to get by simply nicking potatoes from the neighbours without them noticing. Lillian broke down in tears and wrapped her arms around her shoulders – she looked very pretty when she did that. I decided to get back to a once favourite hobby of mine – street busking. Having refreshed my memory with some chords and lyrics, I went to play on the Underground.

Nansen's solution was a more direct one. He proposed scouting for food behind cafés and similar establishments, where the staff put black rubbish bags out on the street at the end of the day. These were often filled with sandwiches and other edible stuff. He knew that Starbucks (whose name sounds truly ridiculous translated in any other language[12]) produce delicious and healthy food for all tastes, and often from organic sources. As soon as the expiry date approaches, all that deliciousness is packed into black rubbish bags for the rubbish men to pick up from the street, thus providing a solid feeding base for local squatters. Unfortunately, Leyton has never really been a middle-class area, so we struggled to find anything. Local supermarkets also didn't seem to be too supportive of our cause – all the bins were hidden behind gates and barbed wire. So our only chance was to go scavenging around small off-licence shops on the high street.

And so one night, off we went on a raid to check all the bins from our house down to the Leyton station. We invited Lillian to come with us, but she refused. She definitely wasn't *that* kind of girl. We didn't care. I think males are less tolerant to hunger than females are.

We checked bin after bin until right on the spot where Leyton High Road makes a turn and meets Church Road we hit the jackpot. A black wheelie bin was full to the brim with fruit and vegetables, as well as Diet Coke cans, so we opened our rucksacks and started loading up. Finally, we would be able to chase hunger away for a while. We should have enough food to survive several days. Needless to say, the thought brought with it a slight taste of victory.

The loud booming of hip hop bass right next to us attracted our attention. A Mustang convertible drew up beside us. The two Black fellas inside watched us, nodding their shaven heads in rhythm with the music and smiling. This was clearly a show they

---

[12] Just try French, Spanish or any other lingo you might be familiar with, and you'll see I'm right.

didn't get to enjoy every day! After we had put the last can in our bags, our audience laughed, clapped and cheered. Then, with a roar from the powerful engine, they disappeared into the night.

Screw you, we thought. At least we have something to eat tonight.

When we spread our loot out on the table at home, the bright light of the kitchen lamp revealed some damage to it. Shopkeepers aren't stupid and throw cucumbers out only after they have started rotting from both ends. Lillian, however, wasn't taken aback by such a small issue. Once the food was out of the bin and delivered, she happily chopped the dripping green rot off the cucumbers, sliced away the white fluffy growth on the tomatoes, diced the rest and mixed up a nice salad. As if by magic our fridge shelf, so empty most of the time, was filled to the top with Diet Coke cans – so many, in fact, that not all of them would fit on our shelf and we had to put some of them on the neighbours' shelves too. It must have been a real surprise for them the next day.

However encouraging the first night's success might have been, we could not rely on bins alone. Somebody had to pay our rent and top up the phones, in case jobs started turning up. Every morning we started with the same ritual of going through all the job advertisements in the Evening Standard and calling about almost any vacancy. Most of them were put there by agencies. They simply wrote down your details and promised to call you back later – they were getting ready for the spring, when things would really get busy in the construction game. And so we phoned them twice a day – first thing in the morning, then around four, hoping that there might be a request for the next day.

To make ends meet, I started busking more seriously. For quite a while my musical activities were the only income for all of us, but clearly that wouldn't be enough. The rent was forty pounds a week each, but I was only making about five pounds an hour. New Year's Eve was just brilliant; in about one and a half hours, people in silly party hats threw into my guitar case more than fifty pounds. Admittedly, a couple of days later on the same spot I made less than two quid in three hours. That's festival economy for you.

Finally, Lillian got a job as a waitress in some place across town. She had to be at work at 6:00 a.m., and there were no trains early enough for her to get there on time, so she would change three buses every night. She was paid thirty pounds per shift. After deductions for rent, travel card and phone top-up, there was nothing left.

On the good side, she ate at work, which was a huge relief for all of us. On the realistic side, the early mornings were turning her more and more into a zombie.

Soon I learned that desperation and helplessness have a certain rhythm attached to them. From Monday to Friday you make calls, greedily grab the newspapers, then look for ads in the windows of convenience stores and so on. The nervousness is mixed with hope and anticipation. Saturdays and Sundays are the worst because there is nothing useful you can do, unless you visit Nine Elms or Petticoat Lane to buy some cheap vegetables or check out stolen tools. But what's the point in looking at tools you can't even buy?

Ever since my arrival, I had felt like I was hitting one rock bottom after the other, going deeper and deeper. You might think this was bad – but wait for it, it was worse. Have you heard the fairy tale about a frog that fell into some cream and whisked it till the cream turned into butter and he had something to step on and jump out? Suddenly, this story acquired new dimensions in my consciousness. Quite frankly, I felt shitty. I was also tortured by dreams about home, family and friends. At night, the light came into my window from the Lea Bridge Road, and now and then an ambulance or a police car would storm down the street with its sirens on, or a night bus would rumble loudly when stopping at the traffic lights. Most nights I would toss and turn in bed until I heard Lillian get up, walking blindly along the corridor and stepping on squeaky old floorboards. Half-three, I would think in despair as I stared at the ceiling. A bit later the pigeons would start to make noises on the window sill, getting ready for sunrise some two hours later.

My parents called me regularly and demanded that I come back. Money was needed to pay for the nursery, apparently even the firewood in our place was about to run out, but I was marooned in London. My debts had grown astronomically, and I wouldn't have the slightest chance of paying them off if I were to return home now. This had turned out to be a one-way ticket, baby.

I wrapped tighter in the blanket and forced myself to shut off the stream of thoughts in my head. I just needed a job, that was all. There were no other real needs for the moment.

Just a job would do to make me happy. Just a little job.

Chapter 3

So far the agencies had not paid any attention to my person, but one day a miracle happened – I made a call and not only did somebody pick up at the other end of the line, but they also offered me some bricklayer's work. Super! All I needed was to borrow, buy or steal some tools, and finally everything could get started! I spent my last phone credit on calling everyone I knew to find a trowel and a bolster. The Ukrainians kindly lent me a hammer.

My understanding of the bricklayer's trade was quite unfocused and contained not so much understanding as rather an abundant lack of any. My employer, Moses Kwaku, was on much the same level, however. His intended business was property development – he would buy an old house, refurbish it, and then sell it for a profit. As a plan it was brilliant, but it would only work if he had at least some idea about how building work should be carried out. Moses Kwaku was from Ghana, as was his wife Cilia, who also worked on the building site, moving around materials and rubbish and keeping an eye on the workers. He was a small, skinny, fifty-something with short grey hair. She was a stunningly beautiful woman with massive eyes and perfect teeth, which shone when she smiled. Her body had lost some of its shape because of the countless childbirths she had been through. With her in the background, Moses seemed to be about three times smaller than he seemed when on his own.

I saw Moses and Cilia every day. They would bring materials and later on collect the kids from school and bore them to death on the building site because there obviously wasn't enough money to hire a nanny. I never knew how many children they had. Once in a while one of them would turn up at the site to bring packed lunch, and it was almost always a different one, though they all had the same shiny eyes. Cilia often mentioned the names of other offspring whom we hadn't had a chance to see yet. She loved to talk, especially about children and God. Both Moses and Cilia spoke the most marvellous, enchanting English I had heard so far. It was percussive and energetic, yet beautifully melodic at the same time.

The building site comprised a typical London two-storey house, which was about to fall apart due to age and neglect, and smelt of wet cement and sawdust. I was commissioned to brick up the fireplaces and a few holes in the walls. The only people with any idea of what should be going on, construction-wise, were a young Englishman called Paul and his pal Demetrio from Athens. Paul was a carpenter and Demets, a sparky. Of all the workers on the site, only they managed to build things so that they looked plumb and level. Neither I nor the Polish gang of dry-liners and plasterers were able to meet their work standards. No kidding – they must both have done similar work before. Perhaps that was why Paul demanded his pay at the end of the week in such a loud and confident voice.

Both I and the Polish guys were very well aware that we were being exploited big time. The Englishman and his Greek friend were the only ones to receive money in an envelope – maybe so the rest of us wouldn't find out what a fair payment should be, or maybe because, unlike us, they also had some official paperwork attached to their cash, paperwork we had no understanding about.

Our first payday finally arrived. The atmosphere was electric. The whole site was vibrating in anticipation and it felt almost as if a big festival was about to burst out in the streets and everybody was a member of a salsa band. Boards and bricks flew in the air, and the Greek electrician turned his little radio, covered in dust and scratched beyond any recognition of the brand, all the way up. Even though my Polish wasn't good at all, it was easy to guess from the chatter of the dry-liner gang that they could already see the pub from there.

Though we all felt like leaving early, Moses, on the contrary, went for a strategy of financial procrastination. For Moses, this was a truly heartfelt moment, when he had to tear out of his flesh and soul the pennies of our salaries. He didn't turn up till half-four to prevent us from leaving too early with the money, as we surely would have done if we had the cash. Together with him was his wife and a weird fellow in his mid-thirties, with a white suit, single-buttoned, over a massively protruding stomach, an eighties hairdo (short top, longish at the back) and cold and glassy eyes. At first, I thought that the chap was completely stoned – he spoke slowly, in a high-pitched voice, stretching his words and sounding a bit like a politician on downers or something. They discussed the upcoming snagging and plumbing; apparently, cheap plumbers weren't available even during the low season. A great deal of their conversation took place in the kitchen, where I was trying to get a grip on the brickwork between the door opening and the window. No matter how I tried, at least one of the parameters was always wrong, and even though the wall I had built wasn't that big, it most definitely exhibited a tendency towards slouching out as a big pot belly on both sides simultaneously – one belly on the inside, the other on the outside, one above the other. Ideally, I would have destroyed it and started again, but I couldn't afford to with my boss, his wife and the weird-looking guy all standing right next to me. So I just put on a performance with the spirit level and a thoughtful facial expression. If they were going to stick around much longer, I decided, I would try to win some time by measuring everything up again. The brickwork was definitely a cock-up by Latvian standards; however, I was relying on the countless stories I had heard about the low demand for quality of work in Britain and on the tales I had been told about Moses's incompetence. Besides, measuring up always looks good, especially if you grab a pencil from behind your ear and start to calculate something on a plasterboard off-cut. In British construction schemes, a pencil behind the ear is how you tell a tradesman from a labourer.

At one point, the white-suited guest of the Kwaku family produced a big bunch of cash from his pocket and gave it to Moses, who immediately passed it over to his wife. The men continued to discuss the colour of the kitchen wall tiles and where they were going to get a stove from, while she split the bills into separate piles and divided one of these – a noticeably bigger one I thought – between two envelopes and wrote something on them. As it turned out later, that was Paul's and Demetrio's share. Envy stung me in the guts. We might all till and plant, yet not everybody gets the same share of the harvest.

Looking back at it now, I can see I scarcely deserved my share of the loot. Honestly. At that stage in my career, I was barely an apprentice. Yet the hopes were high, as were the needs.

The lads started cleaning up and putting their tools away in big steel chests with massive padlocks. Paul and Demetrio covered the windows up with ply and Cilia finally started to give out the wages, approaching each of us separately and pulling the money out of her pocket in exactly the right amount for each person, as if she was a magician. Even though I knew she had counted the right amounts out already, it still looked impressive – how had she managed not to mix up the piles while they were in her pocket?

I was finally freed from my necessity to perform the role of the bricklayer, and what a good feeling that was! Let me tell you what it's like, if you haven't been a builder yourself. Your arms are painfully stretched by heavy weights; your shoulders throb. You throat fills with irritating dust. Your nostrils become fully blocked with sand and cement. The tendons in your back tighten and become as hard as a tabletop. And it hurts; my whole body was aching from working so strenuously and the unfamiliarly humid English weather.

We rushed to the narrow hallway by the entrance. Paul stood there, keys in hand, and waited till everyone was ready to leave. The eyes of men were bright in anticipation of a cold refreshing drink, the drink that would wash away all the bitterness of life. At that moment, the weirdo appeared at the top of the staircase, between dirty, mould-covered brickwork on one side and the black skeleton of an ancient timber stud wall decorated with fluffy wisps of rock wool on the other. An arm in a white sleeve shot up, and a narrow ray of light coming through a gap in the roof threw a small reflection off the precious stone in his ring.

"Thank you, guys. Have a nice weekend, and God bless," he said softly. He closed his hands together in front of his crotch, much like Hitler in official photos, and looked down on us, head cocked to one side. Either side of him emerged Moses and Cilia Kwaku, both smiling. There was something very dignified in this trinity, the man in the white suit in particular.

We murmured a few words of gratitude and hurried out. I hadn't earned a pub visit yet – my wages would barely cover the rent for me and Nansen. True, we had some ten pounds left after the payment, but those were meant for food.

The following week my bricklaying skills improved a bit, so I was paid a little more and even sent fifty pounds to Latvia. It had taken me a month and a half, but finally, I had managed to send some money home. That did not mean that my financial situation had improved much – my debts were still choking me, but at least Armand had found a job for himself, and so was happy to wait for repayment. It was getting warmer, and even Nansen managed to find a couple of odd jobs through agencies.

The 'classmate scheme' continued to work, and soon we had another ex-classmate of ours staying for a couple of days in our little house in Leyton. None of us had any money; all we could help him with was advice, really. In this case, the advice was: bad timing, mate. Agris had arrived with two-hundred pounds and was deeply convinced there would be lots of work available and that the pay would be beyond his wildest imaginings. (That his imagination was pretty wild already goes without saying.) We pulled tired faces in response to his declamations, finished off the beer he had brought, ate our cheap pasta with the cheapest ketchup and told him we were off to bed because we had to get up early in the morning. By London standards, we added, his two-hundred pounds was nothing.

Agris turned sour for a moment, but then he grabbed the phone and rang Latvia to borrow more. We left him to it and went off to sleep.

When I came back home the next day, Agris was gone. The Ukrainians said he had found some other friends who had promised him work.

Back at work, it seemed that Paul wasn't particularly happy about the way I had bricked up around the window and door openings, judging by the swearing I heard when he had to plane down the frames, sometimes to a dramatic difference in thickness. He had been brought up as a gentleman, though, and it never turned personal. Moses, meanwhile, was happy with my low financial requirements and therefore turned a blind eye to the quality I delivered, especially when I agreed to wait for payment until three days later two Fridays in the row. Paul and Demetrio moaned, while the Poles and I kept to ourselves. I didn't have any other choice, though it meant embarrassing conversations with the landlord. One after another four weeks slowly passed and I finally finished all of my tasks, and the Polish gang also finished theirs.

Friday was when we were supposed to receive the biggest wages so far; it was also from that day that our services were no longer needed. Somewhat predictably, on that fateful Friday, Moses once again paid only a part of the salary, feeding us a promise to pay the rest later. A dark, desperate feeling hung over me and the Polish gang like a black, wet blanket. We had already seen things like this in our home countries. As soon as they saw no further use for you, they threw you away and nobody was really interested in handing out the full payment anymore. I bet the phenomenon was as common in Poland as it was in Latvia.

But they weren't going to get away with it here. Demetrio stormed through the house like a hurricane, tearing the electric junction boxes and switches off the walls with Paul's crowbar, and pulling out the cables he had been putting in the ceiling that very morning. Paul drove his van right up to the door and began to throw tools inside, both his and his mate's. Cilia grabbed another of her offspring and disappeared into the garden, leaving the solution up to her husband.

Moses leaned against the kitchen wall, put a hand upon his heart, and asked for water in a dramatic voice. "I shouldn't be talkin' about money. I get a 'eart pain when I do that," he exclaimed.

Demetrio hissed a prediction about the whereabouts of the pain he would feel next time, when somebody inserted a cement mixer there. Together with Paul he quickly collected the sockets, switches and cables in cardboard boxes, but then the two of them got wedged shoulder to shoulder in the narrow hallway. Moses stepped forward and threw on the table what must have been the last and strongest ace up his sleeve, his crowning argument.

"If you leave now, I will have to spend money on advertisements for new people!" He exclaimed, fingers spread over his chest.

Paul barked something particularly vivid, which I found shocking even though at that time my English wasn't particularly good. With a big push, the two of them shot out of the building, jumped in the van and disappeared. Being less confident than the others, I packed my bag silently and took myself off, while

Moses tried to explain it all to the Poles. Poor folks, wasn't this just what they had been fleeing from when they left Poland? And here it all was again – they still had to fight for every last crumb off the table, a task made even more difficult because they could barely speak more than a few English words between the four of them.

I, on the other hand, knew I had almost no chance whatsoever of improving my situation because all the bricklaying was done. So I simply walked to the bus stop, recalculating my expenses on the way. It was a painful fact that I had about a hundred and twenty pounds less than promised. Still, it was a wonderful day, the sun was shining in a particularly bright and friendly manner, and the squirrels seemed to be possessed by hormonal outbursts triggered by the onset of spring. They watched me as I passed through their realm of trees and front hedges. One playful individual ran up a wall like Spiderman and checked out a bird feeder beside a bedroom window. I shrugged, smiled at them, and went home.

After all the time I had spent in England so far, I had experienced only desperation, hard work and a feeling that I had reached a depressing dead end to my life. The salaries were only slightly above those I could have got in Latvia. The price of living gulped greedily whatever profit there might have been, and I was getting no richer than a cat and dog-fighting, bird feeder and rubbish bin-checking, nervous squirrel. The beautiful legend about the ideal job – where you don't have to do anything much but everybody pats you on your shoulder and calls you a good chap for doing it – was fast losing its credibility. It seemed that Armand and other storytellers had made it all up.

And right at this moment of vicious, visceral and vile emotional and financial deprivation of the whole immigration adventure – yes, right then, as it usually happens in all good books sold from good booksellers – the gods gave me a taster of a magical, truly British job. The company Armand was working for finally got its greedy, calloused builders' hands on a very big job indeed – a pharmaceutical factory. The very next day we were on the starting line at six o'clock in the morning, squeezed into Armand's tiny car at the factory gate.

Goodness gracious, as they say. Those were quite spectacular weeks ahead of me.

The large factory on the outskirts of town contained labyrinths of corridors and pipes, mysterious little rooms illuminated by control panels, and massive halls the size of multi-storeyed houses, with walls adorned with ladders, stairs, cages and metal galleries, even more impressive than in Stephen King's *Green Mile*. A couple of rooms had large holes in the floor with metal fences around them – completely mysterious structures. Because of the refurbishment works, all the pipes, big or little, had to be wrapped up in plastic dustsheets so the painters could paint the walls and ceilings. And we cleaned up the dust, too, and unwrapped the old dustsheets. In general, however, there was nothing much to do at all, mainly just to look busy.

The first day was particularly memorable.

"Do you see this board?" I was asked by my Albanian supervisor, a jack of all trades with a thin moustache and eyes so sad you might think he worked for a funeral company.

We were standing in a massive hall with steel walls and no windows. There was nothing there except a single board in one corner. The place felt intimidatingly big and lonely.

I said yes, I could see it. It was a simple wooden plank, perhaps left behind by a forgetful scaffolder.

"If someone comes, pick it up and bring it across the room. Diagonally. And don't rush. The delivery hasn't arrived yet, so we have to kill some time."

Indeed, later in the shift, two managers came in to have a look. You could tell straightaway that they were pharmacologists, pill-makers, not builders. They obviously had no clue about painting or cleaning. Neither had I, but I had an edge – I was here to fight for a better life. I picked the board up and carried it across the room – diagonally and slowly – and carefully laid it down in the kitty corner. Praise the Lord, they left as soon as I put it down.

Later they came by one more time, so I returned the board to where it was before. Slowly, and diagonally.

They paid us hourly. Armand's boss received one-hundred and thirty pounds for each worker, for an eight-hour shift. He paid us eighty. His customer constantly demanded more and more workers because – guess what – at the higher end of the food chain, the masters of the pharmacy business had agreed to pay one-hundred and eighty a day for each individual working in the factory, and they didn't care about the numbers. Eventually, the workers themselves started to look for others to join them, to satisfy the demand. The newcomers had to share with everybody up the chain, so if you brought another worker in you got twenty quid per day from his salary added to yours, thus leaving the newcomer a bare sixty a day. Did that stop the newcomers from earning their pound? No! They, in turn, lured in even more people, and those then really were the ultimate prey who suffered from this example of the process of natural selection, as cold and indifferent as the universe itself. All they had left from the fat one-hundred-eighty a day was a lean forty pounds a shift, after every parasite in its ecological niche had had a bite.

Armand, by the way, officially received three times eighty pounds a day – for him, me and Nansen – because, unlike him, we were illegals. Most of our income went to pay back the debts anyway, but we certainly enjoyed the feeling of the debts diminishing rather than growing.

From day one there was tonnes of work doing nothing in particular. We arrived at 7:00 a.m. and roamed the corridors and rooms with rolls of masking tape and dustsheets in our hands, as if there was something to do. We pretended to be busy all the time and told each other jokes and funny stories. Most of us were from Latvia and Ukraine, except for a couple of lads from Georgia, so we had no problems with communication whatsoever – all these were states of the former Soviet empire and we were all taught Russian at school.

In the whole factory refurbishment enterprise, there was only one Englishman involved, and that was because he had a Latvian friend who got him the job. Tall and with abundant scarlet in his round cheeks, John learned Latvian and Russian swearwords with enthusiasm. It was easy to discover his location by listening for a voice swearing the same way we did, but with an unusual accent. Often he would stand in the middle of the room, legs wide apart and head thrown back, apparently observing with excitement the fluorescent tubes on the ceiling with the sweat running down his face and painting dark patches on the back of his shirt. He loved talking, and the less somebody was able to understand him, the more he talked. His favourite line was 'Your English is better than my Latvian (Ukrainian, Georgian, Russian, etc.)'. For the rest of the time, he would yell pointlessly – but, nevertheless, loudly –'pista vista!' It had become his favourite expression since learning that in Latvian it means 'fucking chicken'.

Then came the night shifts. Oh yes. They paid me a hundred and twenty pounds per shift. This was the legend zoomed in on to a complete close-up. We were polishing steel doors with vinegar, to make them shine, and cleaning up after the painters, sealant applicators, and sparks had gone home. Sometimes, when the boredom was really about to choke us to death, we would fill up dustpans in two different rooms, then swap the locations, throw the dust back on the floor, and sweep it up again to convince the supervisors we were doing a good job.

In case you don't know, every English building site has two sacred moments, each about half an hour long. One happens usually around eleven, the other one around four o'clock. These comprise two breaks lasting half an hour each, when you can pause to enjoy a sandwich and tea. The respect given to these breaks on the stroika reminded me of the attitude some people have towards their country's flag or the singing of a national anthem – and I am not exaggerating. On every building site, especially if it is as big as ours was, workers always try to arrive for their break a bit earlier than everyone else to avoid queuing up in long lines for the tea, and then be able to relax at the table for a little longer. Our half-hour breaks were never shorter than forty-five minutes. Sometimes, when we found a particularly interesting topic of conversation, the breaks would last over an hour. Talking about the rhythm of the work, once three of us spent a whole morning from seven to eleven putting two brushes, a can of paint and a roll of masking tape in order on the shelf in a shed. Armand and I cleaned a brush each, and Misha Krasko stirred the paint so it would not form a film on the top. It was a fantastically well-paid four hours, from seven till the tea break, most of it spent telling jokes and interesting stories.

In three weeks my debts were paid off and my balance was now nil. Never before had nil had such a high value in my life. Since that moment, things became irreversibly better and better. We didn't see much daylight, but we were so tired that we weren't interested in it anyway. Our nights were spent wandering around in the maze of eerie pipe rooms and sterile, hellish–looking kitchen-like spaces, holding a roll of masking tape or a broom. We took on as much overtime as we could and bored ourselves to death with it. The contractors told the company that more workers were needed, and still the pharmacists didn't mind. The call went out for yet more workers to come and soon all our friends and neighbours were involved. So it went on for a few more weeks. We discovered new buildings and corridors, attached paper tape and took it off again, dusted, retold old jokes and drank gallons of tea during our long rest breaks.

And then everything ended. A couple of the best workers were kept for snagging but the rest were sent home. I felt thankful for it. I had paid off my debts, sent enough money to Latvia to take care of all the bills back home, and still had about two-thousand pounds left. It was the first two-thousand I'd ever had in my life – money that I did not have to spend on necessities either, because for the first time all the necessities had been paid for.

Income. What a nice sound that word has.

For the first time in many weeks I woke up at six in the afternoon and instead of rushing to work took a slow walk down to the off-licence and bought some beer – a couple of bottles of decent stuff, not the disgusting cans of frothy piss we usually drank, and then took a bath, another luxury I had never had the time for just ten hours ago. My dusty clothes fell on the floor. I uncorked a Speckled Hen and slid into the hot water. It would be nice to wash those clothes one of these days; I made a sleepy mental note to myself. I hadn't washed any of my two pairs of trousers or three t-shirts since our job at the factory had kicked off.

Relaxation hit me hard and overwhelmingly, like a boxer's fist under the ribcage. I found myself in a dark abyss of happy thoughtlessness and non-sensation even before half of the bottle was finished.

Suddenly the black nowhere where my soul was resting was penetrated by a series of revoltingly loud and unpleasant squeaky beeps. They grew in volume and length, hammering in my head as John might have done with his vinegar bottle for steel polishing. 'Fucking chicken!' I could almost hear him yelling in my face. I opened my eyes. The bath had run cold and the phone in my trouser pocket on the floor was vibrating convulsively from an incoming call.

41

Chapter 4

One of the first things any immigrant must do in London is purchase a phone. This simple act not only enables you to keep in touch with your social contacts but also opens up the jobs market, which in turn is highly dynamic and requires immediate reactivity. Yet, right then, I only wished for the bastard thing to shut up and leave me alone. It did, but then in a few seconds it went off again. Finally, I fished it out and looked at the screen. Moses.

"'Ello, 'ow are you?" He was being unusually friendly. "Listen, do you want to earn some money tomorrow? We need to lift 'igher the level of the basement screed. It 'as to be done very quickly, so I want you to make some plywood shutterin' for me."

That was weird. I was supposed to be a bricklayer, after all. Wouldn't it be better if he asked Paul? I inquired.

"Paul is workin' in Oxford at the moment and can't come ovah. As a brickie, you have experience with foundations and stuff, so you can 'elp. I'll pay you seventy pounds a day."

Now this was truly peculiar. The sum was simply unbelievable for this particular employer, especially taking into account the way we had parted the last time. I did some calculations. If I could make seventy pounds before Monday that would help to pay the rent, top up the phone and even buy some food for the next week – and my two thousand quid would remain intact. I loved the idea. The only problem was, I didn't quite know how to make shuttering. I gave it a quick second thought, and then decided that it shouldn't be too much of a problem.

"What about the money you still owe me?"

"Everythin' will be paid. I was gonna call you about that anyway (ha, tell me, Mr Scrooge). I 'ave paid Paul and the rest of the guys everythin', so tomorrow I will make it a hundred and ninety pounds. A hundred and ninety."

Well, that meant a whole lot of rent, enough for more than a week, and still something left over. Mmmmmmm. Something fishy was going on here, but I let it be. Money was *über alles* right now.

"And what if I have to work for more than a day?"

Silence. Then:

"You will receive everythin' you earn, in full. I promise and I apologise for the delay."

I got out of my cold bath and made some calls until I happened to hit upon somebody who was able to explain what shuttering was. As it turned out, shutterers are people who build plywood boxes to be filled in with concrete – for pillars, for example, or concrete stairs. I then borrowed from Misha a cordless drill, an electric saw and a hammer, and next morning I returned to the job I had last been on over a month before.

The house seemed to be almost fully refurbished now. A touch of paint was still needed here and there and the furniture was assembled only partially, with some already ready, other bits still waiting in big IKEA boxes piled up in the living room. Moses took me through the house into the garden and showed me a backdoor entrance into the basement. It still had bare hinges and no doors.

"Our customer decided at the last minute to have a much 'igher floor level in 'ere. Concrete floorin'. We need you to build a ply wall across, so that the concrete won't come out over that line. Also, between this room and the one next to it, where the boiler is. We want to raise the floor 'ere four feet."

My understanding of building work was still quite uncertain, but it all seemed very odd to me. If the floor was raised more than a metre anyone coming in would have to walk almost on all fours. The room was quite small anyway, some three by four metres. Moses suddenly looked nervous and fetched his wallet out of his pocket.

"I will pay what I owe you right now, and the other seventy this afternoon."

Plywood sheets and timber had been heaped up right outside the basement, next to a big pile of fresh ballast sand. I glanced back at the house, at the painfully familiar wall under the kitchen window, which still had that pot belly, and plugged in the skill saw.

My first attempt in the trade of chippentry didn't seem to go too badly. When I look back at it today, however, I realise there could have been a lot to complain about, especially if somebody decided to check it all with a spirit level. I screwed in my last screw around three o'clock and when I lifted my eyes Moses was standing right over me. It almost felt as if he had been hiding in the bushes all the time, watching me. I wasn't used yet to the cordless drill, so some of the joints looked terrible. On the other hand, the whole construction was meant to be removed a few days later after the concrete was in, so I figured that was why Moses didn't object to anything. He didn't even complain about the fact that I had wasted so many screws, which came as a surprise and a relief. I received my money and was shown the way out, in a bit of a hurry, or so it seemed to me. I asked if there would be any more jobs in the foreseeable future. Moses said he'd call me back. By that time, I already knew that in England that usually meant there would be no call, so I simply went home.

Upon my return, I discovered that I must have left the charger for Misha's cordless drill at the site. I tried to reach Moses on the phone a few times, but it was switched off. *Oh well*, I thought as I stretched out on the bed, *there was nothing much I had to do the next day so I could probably get back into that garden somehow and retrieve the charger myself.*

I definitely wasn't in the mood to do anything right away and I didn't feel like getting up early either, so I did not leave the house until late Sunday afternoon. I hadn't slept so long and so well for an eternity, and even the fact that I had to go back and get Misha's charger didn't strike me as too much of a problem. The rare but fast Sunday buses took me bouncing along on their seats, which were festooned with Saturday night's chips and burger wrappings, through the streets of East London to Canning Town, where I had to walk the remaining distance to the house. The sun was shining, and if you weren't in the shade you had to take your jacket off to avoid sweating too much. It was a beautiful day and even though it was only the end of January, some tree branches already had little green dots that would soon become proper buds.

Knock, knock on the recently painted door with its shiny brass Yale lock. No reply. The front of the house was still full of timber and plasterboard off-cuts and there were grey streaks on the pavement where somebody had moved cement bags around. The wind caught a piece of paper cement bag and tossed it playfully into the front garden next door. I knocked once more just to be sure and then approached the small gate leading to the garden, where residents would put their wheelie bin out. It had a lock on it, but it felt justifiable in this case not to pay too much attention to normal standards of social behaviour. A quick jump over the gate and I landed in the sticky mud on the other side. The lazy bastards had left the spring cleaning of the garden for the tenants.

The basement still had no door but the concrete was in place. Next to the entrance there was a dirty concrete mixer, barrel pointing downwards as if it was crying for something or simply in a sad mood. When I say 'dirty', I mean somebody had used it and not rinsed it afterwards with the result that little concrete icicles now hung from the inside of the drum and had formed a small pool of concrete below. Remarkably, the mixer looked brand new. I walked through the basement space, still being puzzled by the decision to pour in so much concrete. Misha's charger was lying under something in the corner – it was no wonder I hadn't noticed it. I dropped it in my rucksack, then paused. I saw that a corner of the shuttering I had constructed had given way under the pressure of the concrete mass and come apart, despite the supports that should have kept it in place. The concrete had leaked onto the floor, lowering the level of the floor surface. A whole length of ply had been pushed out of place and was now completely askew. Yeah, I obviously had to work on my technique with a screwdriver. Annoyed with myself, I kicked one of the supports that hadn't done its job and the whole board came off with an unpleasant squeak.

Wait, something funny's going on here. Why on earth would anyone want such a depth of concrete on a basement floor? And what was that lump sticking out of the grey mass? Hadn't they mixed the concrete properly? I kneeled down by the section which had been exposed after I kicked it. The concrete surface was still dark grey and moist, and in it, spooky against the grey background, shone a pale line of what looked for all the world like a length of bone, still covered with skin. Like the doubting Thomas, I poked at it incredulously with my finger then withdrew it hastily. It was, without a doubt, a human leg. The flesh was cold and stiff, but unmistakably of human origin. The skin close to the knee was slightly dented where it had rested against a screw sticking out of the plywood.

I got back up and looked around, my heart in my mouth. The stone cold concrete cube in front of me was silent. I wondered how many bodies you could stick in such a place, and almost threw up, but managed to swallow hard, to avoid leaving traces on the scene. It was high time I sodded off.

Chapter 5

I cleared the gate in one go and was at the bus stop in no time. As soon as I had collapsed onto the bus seat, my legs went as limp as a pair of dead fish and it felt like I'd never be able to get myself up again. I thought feverishly about what I'd discovered. It seemed I had helped to hide a corpse, or maybe even several corpses – who could tell? – With my own two hands. Should I call the police? It was a risky option. The most likely consequence would be Her Majesty the Queen paying for my ticket back home and me being blacklisted, which would eliminate any chance of returning in the future. Besides, the whole crime scene was literally covered with my fingerprints. What if I left everything as it was? Then there would always be a possibility that somebody would exterminate me as a witness. Sooner or later Moses would come back and notice the leg sticking out of the floor, as cold and stiff as the concrete enclosing it. Although, on second thoughts, he didn't know either my full name or where I lived, only my pay-as-you-go phone number. But it was the same number I gave to all the agencies. If I changed it, no one will be able to reach me about jobs. Bugger.

My first instinct was obviously to go straight back to Latvia, especially now I had earned some dough. I dwelt upon the prospect as I changed from one bus route to the next. It was a lovely spring day but despite this and even though I knew from the internet that it was snowing in Latvia the desire to quit my gold-digger's adventure and go home grew stronger and stronger.

When I entered the house I was hit by a pungent smell. Immediately the vision of the pale and cold flesh of a corpse flashed before my eyes, but I shrugged it off. This smelled more like an unwashed urinal rather than rotting meat. I took off the shoes and entered the living room, where the source revealed itself. It was Agris, the ex-classmate who had appeared briefly amongst us not so long ago. It was him all right, though his cheeks were now covered in lush facial hair, his eyes were bulging and red, and he was giving off the sweaty aroma of a homeless. He was sprawled at the dining table, breathing like a faulty steam engine and wolfing down chicken soup served up by Misha.

"I found him in Stratford," Misha said, looking fondly at Agris as if he was a family cat, lost and found again. "Had to bring him home and feed him some chicken."

Agris waved hello with a slice of bread and continued eating.

We went into the kitchen.

"Tell him to take a bath," Misha instructed as he opened the window. "My bruv is gonna be here in a minute, and you know how sensitive he can be."

He was right there. Grisha thought of himself more as a historian[13] than a builder and paid more attention to cleaning and cooking than anyone else in the house. He would absolutely hate the smell Agris had brought with him. As if I had nothing else to worry about! Now I had a corpse in a customer's basement, a bum of a classmate and a smartass historian-turned-chippie of a neighbour. Everything seemed to be building up to me getting pissed off big-time in the very near future. I grabbed a Russian Hunter from the fridge – awful beer, but strong – and re-entered the living room where Agris was still eating. Between gulps and slurps, he told me his story.

It began with him being thrown out of the place where he had been promised lodging and work. That was after they had taken his deposit and rent for the first month, with him sharing a room with five other Latvians. What was the rent, we asked. Seventy pounds a week for a room in East Ham. There were twelve other Latvians in the house and no bunk beds. What a rip-off!

After several days he finally got a job in a builders' gang mainly constituted of his housemates. Its leader – who gathered

---

[13] Both brothers Krasko had Master's degrees in history. They weren't from a Western university, though, which rendered them practically useless.

the outrageous rent from everyone – thought of himself as an artisan builder and had the ambition to be an entrepreneur and a site manager simultaneously. Whatever his real talents were, he had no clue about the British building world. He signed contracts on the basis of piece work, not on a daily salary. The poor bastard didn't appreciate that Western European trade unionists had shed their blood, sweat and tears for a good reason – to achieve a better future for themselves and succeeding generations. For, lo and behold, if a British employer does not have to pay for your time, neither does he stress too much about the deliveries being on time. Hence unsuspecting, inexperienced Eastern European twats sit around on the site waiting for deliveries that never come and earn nothing at all. Meanwhile, the rent and billing clock keeps on with its merciless penny-pound, pound-pound tick-tocking. At the end of the day, the job takes at least three times more hours than the builders have estimated. Without the necessary contacts and any understanding on how to order materials, the poor bastards are totally screwed. They have been paying their rent, bills, food and so forth, and when finally received, their wages have lost any glamour and barely cover the expenses invoked while waiting for action.

Extreme times call for extreme measures, so the leader of the gang cancelled the weekly payments but continued demanding the rent, which pushed Agris to borrow again. And again. And then some more. Eventually, when his sponsors in Latvia had to borrow money themselves to be able to send it to him, they rebelled and denied any further credit. Sums required for his London allowance were far above the sums they would normally deal with, and they started accusing him of heroin addiction. Nothing else could explain where so much money could go in such a short time, according to his family. He had tried to discuss matters with the leader in a friendly manner, Agris said, but instead he had been beaten up and thrown onto the street.

There a new life started for him. He lost his phone after the first night on a park bench and couldn't remember where our house was; and we were his only other contacts in the whole of the UK. There was no point in returning to Latvia as it would take most of the eternity to earn enough to pay his debts back. He ate the food disposed of in black rubbish bags by cafés and off-licences at night and earned a little pocket money begging for used travel cards at underground stations and reselling them for a couple of quid later. In the pre-Oyster era, this used to be quite a business, especially among Jamaicans. A couple of times he almost got hotted up for entering someone else's territory but eventually settled down in Stratford, sleeping in parks and along the river Lea. One might think it strange that we didn't notice him earlier, but then there are nine million people in London, according to official statistics, and if you count squatters and illegal immigrants not on the electoral roll, it must be quite a few more. And big cities alienate people, after all.

Be that as it may, he had also done something useful for himself. He had some acquaintances living in Ireland and somehow had managed to find their mobile numbers through common friends in Latvia. Not only that, he had also called them from a pay phone, using the money earned on ticket touting.

"I can stay at their place," he said, wiping the soup off his beard and licking his fingers one by one. "They say it is much easier to find a job over there than it is in London. All I need is thirty quid to get from here to Dublin. The trains run on winter tariffs now. In any case, I need to get outta here. I can't stand it anymore. People are too scary around here. I think everybody wants to murder me. No, seriously. Everybody smiles at me and asks me how I am. I'm not an idiot; I know they don't care at all how I am. Not *at all*. I tried to answer a few times but they just ignored the answer! But they keep on asking regardless. And then the *smiling*! It is simply not possible that *everybody* should have a reason to smile at me. Plus, they always ask where I'm from. That's because they can spot a foreigner right away and want to snitch on him. They probably have ways to figure out from a person's appearance if they have a business visa or not. My life here is like a horror film, man. Horrible, horrible people."

I took a sip from my can. The tanginess of the yeasty froth helped to lessen the impact of Agris's powerful odour. I saw in him myself as I had been some months earlier. Back then I was convinced, like Agris was now, that everybody in London was a Janus-faced pickpocket and snitcher – for how else could my Latvian brain explain the overload of smiles and polite phrases? What does he want from me, that black geezer at the bus stop, when he starts up a chat about what a tough week it had been for both of us? Maybe he wants to snatch my travel card during the conversation? Please don't think we're racist; it is sadder than that. The system has turned us into xenophobics, and we find it hard to snap out of it. Could it be that all women here are nymphomaniac sluts because they don't avoid your gaze and sometimes even smile in return? It made my head spin at first. In Western Europe, life generally is seen as worth living and everyone is a potential friend. In Eastern Europe, we give strangers a mean look instead. If only we could hang all those Soviet leaders by the balls for that! They stole from us the main value in life – the joy of being alive. They traumatised the brains of several generations, and millions of people are still apprehensive of shadows and see one other as snitchers and enemies. I'm not the first to notice that one symptom of culture shock à la Eastern Europe, in the west is the cramp in the face. Finding ourselves dropped into this culture of smiling, we initially try to be polite and smile like everyone else, but unfortunately, our zygomaticus major is rather inexperienced and undertrained for exercise. We can't keep it up for long. Despite our best efforts, an agonised expression of desperation and pain inevitably shows through.

'How are you?' 'Not too bad. And yourself?' By now, I was starting to get used to this useless ritual. Actually, nobody ever gives a fuck about how you are doing. It is simply considered to be polite to ask. Try to ask 'how are you' in Eastern Europe, and you will be given a whole list of relevant updates, from changes in marital status to medical records. We treat it as a question, not a greeting. The bizarre thing is, as much as we think that the British are impolite in ignoring your answer to a question they have just addressed to us, they consider *us* rude because we don't use 'please' and 'thanks' as often as they do. Let me get this straight: we're not rude. It's just that when we say it, we actually mean it. The same goes for smiling.

You see, in our culture a smile is like a sex toy – it is normally shared behind a closed door and only with people you trust. When was the last time (if ever) that a salesperson, ticket inspector or cab driver smiled at you in Eastern Europe? And don't try to sell me your rubbish about things changing. The thing is, we have been taught by our parents that being grey and close to invisible is the highest virtue and, set on scary cultural autopilot, we hasten to teach the same to our children. In our world, being lower than grass is a survival strategy. Let me tell you how it works. Imagine a crowd of people all of the same size. A big scythe sways about an inch over them. As soon as someone sticks out by being taller, louder, more colourful or anything else, the scythe goes 'CHOP!' and everyone is equal again.

Macabre as this comparison might be, it encapsulates most of Eastern European history. The gene pool of our ancestors was weeded out on the basis of traits like colourfulness and loudness, so there is little potential left in us in that respect. We are genetically programmed to kill ourselves with work, not entertainment. Even today, the worst thing an Eastern European mother can tell her child is to hush it by saying: 'Be silent! Don't you see, everybody is looking at you!'

For us, there is nothing scarier and more humiliating than being looked at. No wonder we feel uneasy when the background expands beyond the spectra of grey.

"Four-hundred euros a week," said Agris, interrupting my inner monologue. "In a car wash in Galway. That's on Ireland's west coast. Simply super, innit?"

I wanted to point out to him that it wouldn't be pure profit because he would still have rent and bills to pay, but I was overtaken by another thought. The only thing Moses knew about me was my nationality. If the corpse in the basement had something to do with the mafia (for some reason I stereotyped a corpse in concrete with the mafia) then, logically, they might be looking for me now in Heathrow or at Victoria coach station. (Back in the day, direct planes to Latvia were rare and they all left from Heathrow.) Buses ran twice a week and were the preferred mode of transportation because of their cheapness and regularity. So in total, there were only two places from which I could leave the country, which made hunting me down relatively easy. As soon as I realised this, a rush of panic surged from my stomach upwards.

"Will, would you go with me to Ireland?" Agris asked suddenly.

Without thinking about it any further, I exclaimed, "Yes!"

He sighed with noticeable relief.

"How unfortunate that I didn't find you while you were on that super job Misha was telling me about. Hey, could you buy me a ticket? I will return the money as soon as I get any."

I could have predicted that, but never mind. You have to help where you can, for the law of karma applies to everybody, and it looked like we would be following a long path together. I forced Agris to take a bath and went to the internet café to check whether a trip to Ireland was really that cheap. It was, a single ticket for thirty pounds and a return for thirty-five. The train was leaving late the next evening.

What could be better than that? I went to Euston Station early next morning, bought the tickets, and took a walk through Regent's Park. Someone had shut off the sunshine and the weather was turning English again. It was chilly and drizzling, but I didn't mind – Regent's Park always sets my soul in harmony. It is truly amazing how they manage to get flowers and bushes there to bloom all the year round. I was happy that the busking had allowed me to get to know London, at least a bit, because as soon as the dream came true and I found a proper job, there would be no free time left to be a tourist anymore.

I bought coffee in a paper cup and chestnuts in a paper bag, and made it to the open field by the zoo fence. Young men full of energy and vigour were playing football, and elderly ladies were walking their silly-looking lap dogs. There was so much positive feeling to all this mundanity. It felt simply unfair to have to flee to Ireland right now. I felt that something inside me had given up resisting and that I had managed to shutter and smash a part of me that used to be important and integral, but turned out, upon closer inspection, to be obsolete. My soul had opened itself up to this city and to a world so different from mine. I remembered the late night rush in Soho, Millennium Bridge in the dark, and the imposing walls of Westminster Abbey, where every brick could tell you a story. Mind you, even Billingsgate fish market was about two hundred years older than the capital city of my country. I liked this place.

I knew I would come back. And to make my comeback secure, I had to do something first.

I made a call from a phone booth to the police and in my best English told them about a corpse in a building site in Canning Town, at such and such address. Without answering their questions (to be honest, at that time I found it extremely difficult to understand English over the phone), I hung up and went back to Leyton to prepare for the journey. I felt like I had done all I had to, and even though I was still a little nervous, the new adventure ahead was spicing it all up. All of a sudden I started to enjoy all this. The minds of young males thrive on adrenaline.

***

The train shot through night-time Britain. As soon as we left London there was complete darkness outside the windows. We tried to relax in our seats and envied those who had money to pay for a night in a bunk bed. Toothbrushes in hand, and dressed in pyjamas, the wealthy paid their evening visit to the toilets. Still, thirty-five quid for a return to Dublin (ferry included) wasn't bad at all. From neighbouring seats, we heard the sounds of the Gaelic tongue for the first time in our lives. I noticed that Irish women have apparently common genetic traits, beautiful expressive eyes and thin lips.

Agris became depressed as soon as he realised he was among suspicious-looking foreigners again and that the only fellow-human being that he saw as predictable and reliable was me. He had changed a lot from the young man full of vitality and ambition who had arrived in London many weeks ago. I remembered so well him yelling across the width of the Lea Bridge Road, "Whatta fuck they write on the road 'LOOK LEFT' for?" Well, that's what they have to do to keep us continental strangers alive, because in the British Isles the cars drive on the left. When you arrive for the first time, this tiny detail comes as more of a surprise than even Big Ben (which is not big at all, disappointingly). Why? Because you weren't prepared for it! Right now, however, the excitement was gone. He had entered a phase of loneliness, sexual hunger and insecurity. Only when I gave him my phone to make a call back home did I understand, from the bravado in his voice, that he was determined not to return a loser. Maybe because they would break his legs for not paying the borrowed money back, I thought, grimly. Or maybe because he wouldn't be able to look in the mirror without shame and self-pity.

All things considered, it was a good decision for both of us to head for the ancient isle of Cuchulain or, as the Irish themselves call it, Eire.

The ticket inspector had a Celtic motif tattooed on his arm, which seemed to be a good omen until he stopped by our seats for a little chat.

"You're gonna love Ireland, it's absolutely brilliant," he told us with an accent I had never heard before. Agris almost crouched under the seat to avoid getting involved in the conversation. Too much familiarity, I guess. Or maybe he was dreading the inevitable next question, "Where are you from?" The knowledge that we were the weakest, most sought-after prey, Eastern Europeans, bloody foreigners and illegal workers, dwelled deep in the very core of our souls. I responded to the man's overtures with reluctance and suspicion and didn't encourage him to linger. What do you care, I felt like asking him. Are you going to denounce us to the Inland Revenue, or what?

I had sent half of my money back home, in case our journey was terminated at the Irish border or pickpockets helped themselves to our cash. Knowing that made me feel easier. I opened a free newspaper and tried to relax. The paper obviously didn't contain anything about the Canning Town corpse as it was too soon, but the disappointment was still there. Still, the distance between me and the Canning Town corpse was currently widening at a rate of almost two-hundred miles per hour. *Uzpriekšu!*[14] They say Ireland is the most Latvian country in the world after Latvia itself, for it currently hosts more than twenty per cent of all people who hold Latvian citizenship. We'd see. I put the paper aside and tried to get some sleep.

Dublin was not a nice place. I remembered McGowan's 'Dirty old town, dirty old town'... dirty indeed. There was no sign of London's glamour or ambitions to be the capital of the world, not in the slightest. We wandered around for a while and then got on the bus to the capital of Connaught, the merry town of Galway.

The little village ten miles away from Galway where Agris's friends were living was experiencing an explosion in growth, at least as far as Latvianisation was concerned. The number of

---

[14] Forward! (Latvian)

Latvian newcomers grew as quickly as the mushrooms they were picking or the houses they were building for the locals. We were allowed to stay in a freshly built two-storey dwelling, which felt like HQ for Tullamore Dew and Jameson whiskey fans, especially at weekends. The men mostly worked in construction or on farms, while the women were more focused on becoming sales assistants or waitresses. Guess now – who do you suppose acquired the better English language skills?

Not the Irish in any case. Not one of them could speak Gaelic anymore, it's true, but their version of English sounded like gibberish to us. As soon as we got our first job, labouring on a local farm, we realised that what we had learned of the language in London was little help under such conditions, and for the first couple of weeks, understanding the Irish accent was like plodding through a swamp. Secondly, as city boys transported to these unfamiliar, rural surroundings, we felt psychologically raped. I mean, it wasn't the amount of work – more the nature of it. We also discovered that there are lots of splinters in a rake handle. Lots, I'm telling you. They stung.

Nevertheless, after our first salary, things started to look up a bit. Our boss, a red-faced chunk of fat with arms almost entirely covered in tattoo ink, was selling flowers. He was damn good at it, I was told – one of the biggest growers in the county. Once we started to get a better grip on things, he let us to do some weeding and look after his greenhouse as well. On top of that, he offered us the chance to live in an old caravan just off-site. There was already one chap, a quiet Ecuadorian with a gold chain around his neck, living in it but we were glad of the change, as there were too many Latvians where we were living and new ones were arriving almost on a weekly basis. Besides, the Ecuadorian had a TV with DVD player and a pile of action films. He even had a real, expensive coffee machine.

Our farmer's improvised shanty town at the back of the potato field contained some five old caravans in different stages of decomposition. There were workers from all over the world, though most were from Latvia and Belarus. Our team contained some fifteen souls, two thirds of whom were working for the flower man and the rest for his son-in-law, who ran a chicken farm. It was unfamiliar territory for me and Agris but we were willing to give anything a try. After three weeks we found out that the flowers would be over soon, even before we had learned the names for the different types. On the other hand, payday was coming, which was good news, as some of us had not been paid for a whole month – me and Agris for two weeks. Our savings were close to spent, so payday was eagerly awaited by us all.

That was when our boss snitched on us, his own workers.

Chapter 6

That Thursday – how remarkable, since Friday was meant to be payday – the fields and the front yard of the farm filled up with cars, some of which had GARDA written on their side, which is Irish for POLICE. It happened around ten in the morning, and there also were a few dogs involved, enjoying a morning's walk and sniffing the immigrants out. Most of the workers got thrown into cars right away; the Ecuadorian got taken straight off the tractor. Agris and I fell flat among the flowerbeds. Luckily, at the time of the ambush, we were some hundred yards off the epicentre of activities, and even the spaniel who sniffed my face and wagged his tail a bit didn't pay any more attention after that and walked back where the detectives were handcuffing a man who thought that resisting and shouting loudly in English would give him some advantage. A true bloodhound, the spaniel headed for the fight rather than attending to two unmoving men.

It was all over in less than twenty minutes. After they had gone, we hid behind the greenhouse and sat around in the bushes and nettles for some two hours more, to be secure. As soon as we reached our caravan, we found our chubby boss browsing through the Ecuadorian's DVDs. The telly and the coffee machine were already in the back of his truck.

The fat bastard expressed his delight and happiness about us saving our asses and paid our salary in full right there and then. He simply took a wad of bills out of his pocket, and that was it. Looking back, it seems to me he was in a celebratory mood and not too bothered about having to pay the two of us. Besides, he took all the stuff the workers had accumulated while living here as the Garda were not interested in any of that. Later, some more experienced folks explained to me that, at the time, no employer was held responsible for hiring people without work permits. None of us had any official papers so the Irish government had the right to arrest us and kick us out of the country, whereas the employer had the right to shrug his shoulders and say: 'What? They didn't have any work permits? They didn't tell me!' And then he could help himself to all the stuff they left behind, including their wages.

As things stood, it was clearly risky to stay there any longer. Before we parted, the Ecuadorian – may the sun shine upon his way back home – had advised us on a good way to get any job for at least a couple months. All you had to do when applying was pretend to be Dutch (nobody speaks Dutch in the British Isles). This would explain why you didn't have any official papers. You would say that you had applied for a National Insurance number and expected it to arrive some time later. This ruse could get you employment in places where workers were really needed, as everybody knew how long the bureaucrats took to send out documents. Once the National Insurance issue became too pressing, you simply moved on to the next farm or other source of work.

We decided to give the scheme a try and to explore the Republic of Ireland at the same time. One of the guys we knew on the farm gave us a lift to the local highway, where we lifted our hands in the international gesture of hitchhiking and got a ride from the second car that turned up. We had escaped from the police, received our salary, held onto our possessions and were now in the company of a very talkative Irishman who bought us lunch on the way. It was a good start! Sometimes, to feel happy, all you need is just a little bit less injustice than usual. The others were less lucky than us, and it made us feel somewhat uneasy – but on the other hand, what could we do about it anyway?

The road before us wound in twists and curves through Oranmore and Ballinasloe, over the slopes of rolling hills that make travelling through inner Ireland so monotonous on one hand yet charming on the other. There were sheep behind the hedgerows; occasionally they even roamed onto the roads and watched the honking cars with curious eyes before moving out of the way with dignity. Between Athlone and Mullingar there were fewer cars, at least on the roads we were on. Our first destination was Mullingar, which – as all Latvians know only too well from the newspapers – is known as the place where most 'mushroom Latvians' find employment on the mushroom farms. Agris had obtained another useful phone number, this time, that of a friend's uncle. There was no job at the moment, the uncle said, but there might be later.

Right, then it is worth to pay a visit, then. With our method of transportation, it could take a couple of days to get there and besides, we always were asking around for jobs in whichever village we found ourselves along the way. The Irish were extremely helpful and welcoming; they would give us phone numbers to try our luck and sometimes even drove us somewhere to meet a friend or a relative who might have vital info about jobs. Yet, despite their best efforts, nothing worked out right away. We never waited for the miracle to happen by itself, just carried on. Once or twice I did a bit of busking to get some pocket money but, as it usually is with little towns, there was very little money to be had. I barely made enough for food. I wouldn't, however, want to diminish the friendliness and helpfulness of the local folks, who were great. I fell in love with the country and its people within the first couple days of our trip.

It wasn't all good news, though. If I were to compare the wonderful people and the picturesque scenery of Ireland to a fragrant ointment, then Agris's attitude provided abundant flies in it. He hated having to pay for hotels, for instance, and tried to talk me into cheating on the hotel owners. I didn't want to take such risks and supported the policy of sleeping outdoors in parks or between motorway carriageways where we would be concealed from unwanted attention. Nobody would ever think of looking for job-seeking Eastern Europeans between the carriageways of a motorway in the first place. On the health and safety side, we performed our infrequent hygienic wash-ups in the toilets of cafés and libraries. The latter we would hit in every town, as they normally offered free internet. We checked our inboxes, sent out a few CVs, and then rinsed our feet and armpits in the lavatory sink. The clothes posed a more complicated issue, as laundries charge for washing and drying, and we felt that to be a luxury we couldn't afford. We reassured ourselves on the grounds that a) when we were hitch-hiking no one could sniff us before we got into their car, by which time it was too late anyway, and b) our undies were covered by our trousers and our dirty socks were safe inside our boots, so they shouldn't smell too bad at least as long as we kept them covered.

Despite our efforts, we kept having breakdowns in communication. Instead of keeping up a nice relaxing chat with the people who were giving us a ride, Agris always sat in the back seat with a face like a dedicated sourpuss, probably reminding drivers of bad American horror movies featuring deranged hitchhikers. Ladies, especially, found him unnerving. He never participated in the conversation, even if he got asked something directly, and pretended he didn't understand English. The only time he became at all lively was when we happened to get a lift from another Latvian. The Latvian had lived around Athlone for a few years and earned his living on roadworks. He and Agris hit it off instantaneously.

"Just look at them Irish," said the Latvian. "They're empty people. They're not interested in anything except beer and football. If you mention ice hockey, no one has a fucking clue. I had to buy a satellite dish with Russian channels on in order to watch a game. And all they fucking do is keep smiling and asking howdafuck are you. As if they care! Bastards. Shit, if only I could, I would smash the snouts of a couple of the wankers!"

Snout-smashing, however, was being constantly postponed because that would jeopardise his employability.

Agris understood the pain of our countryman one hundred per cent and told him that the English were even worse than the Irish. Not only were they empty and posh, they were also imperialists and even once occupied Ireland. So there was something that bound Latvians with the Irish – if not the mentality, then at least something historical, an external imperial enemy. Russia was to us what England was to the Irish, Agris observed. The Latvian agreed, but then pointed out that the entire West was rotten anyway.

"Good luck, boys," the Latvian said as we shook hands on parting. "May we see each other again in our motherland someday, and go for a beer. I got a feelin' I only need to earn a few grand more and then I'll head back home. My Dad's old house is waiting there amid the blue lakes, and the storks, and the dragonflies… Eeh."

I thought I almost saw a tear in his eye, steely and masculine though he seemed.

He never gave us his phone number, however. And what for the storks and dragonflies? I remember him saying he's from Jugla, a rather industrial part of the city of Riga. I guess the Latvia you remember tends to be more beautiful than the Latvia you lived in...

Our trip continued. The Mullingar uncle turned out to be as disenchanting as everybody else. At the moment we finally hit our destination – the free-and-easy town of Mullingar itself, the fungal centre of Ireland – there was no work available. During our stay in the Lakepoint Park, we were woken up by a fondling gay couple in the bushes nearby. Not long after they were done and had left us in peace, a slow rain started. It did not stop till early morning and we had to wring the water out of our sleeping bags before we could put them back in our rucksacks. I'm not sure if it was the smell of our clothes or the overall dampness of the situation that finally persuaded us to count our money again and decide to go posh and take a room at a B&B at the first opportunity.

How amazing it felt. For one thing, the room had tea and sugar for absolutely free! First off, we rinsed our sleeping bags and everything else in the bath and then spread them out around the room before spending the rest of the day in the big lounge watching TV. Isn't it interesting how you reach a stage in your life when just watching TV in a common room and hearing the news of a country that isn't your own can make you feel completely relaxed and comfy? The truth, however, was, that the national news in Ireland was unlikely to mention corpses sunk in concrete on a building site in London. The internet gave no clues about it either. So far I had managed to brush aside my anxiety about the matter, distracted as I was by adjusting to life in a new country, but now I had the chance to relax; I started to think about it again. *What if the police hadn't done anything about my call?* I certainly wasn't brave enough to call them again and find out how they were getting on with the investigation.

I forgot about the corpse I had discovered, however, after we met a couple of great people in that lounge. Unlike us, who were merely attracted by the free cookies and fruit on offer, Antonio and Rahima came downstairs on purpose to watch the football. They arrived with a backpack full of beer and started drinking and cussing right away, while watching the game. Football is a great conversation starter and a good excuse for some boozing. We hadn't had any alcohol for a long time, so it turned out to be a fantastic evening. Red Stripe isn't my favourite, but you don't complain about a beer you haven't paid for.

Antonio was a dark, hairy and massive bloke who waved his hands a lot and kept referring to *cazzo*[15]. His nationality was obvious to anyone who has ever seen an Italian comedy; he was as stereotypical as stereotypes ever get. The way he waved his hands about made it look like he was translating himself into sign language all the time. I had never realised that human hands could be such expressive tools of communication. His girlfriend Rahima was British of Pakistani descent, a second-generation immigrant. She had large dark eyes and a body to die for. When she reached for a beer from the floor, Agris and I had to concentrate hard to keep our eyes focused on the TV, otherwise the fascinating contours of her bust would have driven us cuckoo. Her pretty face was adorned by a couple of piercings, one in the nostril and the other on her chin. On her right shoulder was an aggressive dragon, tattooed in green ink. Whenever Antonio started talking too much bullshit she would sink her long red nails into his stomach and laugh loudly.

Let me get it straight, for the record. It wasn't just our hormones that were responsible for our interest in Rahima. She really looked superb, especially in tight jeans.

When the game was over, it turned out that our new friends also had some spliff to share. We squeezed into their bathroom and shared the joint, getting even higher on the joy of socialising. After a long period of no fun, no alcohol, no sex, no nothing, we didn't need much to be knocked out by drugs. The THC kicked in quickly and somewhat brutishly. Even Agris started to talk. He tried to tell us all a couple of old Russian jokes, but nobody understood them, including me, even though I might have known the original versions. That didn't lessen the amount of fun we were having though.

The neighbours hushed us into bed at around two in the morning. We slept too long and missed breakfast. Our new friends had already left. We made another call to the fungal

---

[15] Cock (not the bird kind). (Italian)

uncle, and then the owner of the place made a couple of calls on our behalf. Yet there were no jobs available just then.

Even the free breakfast the landlady gave us despite getting up late couldn't dissipate what I am tempted to call the Mullingar disappointment. It seemed to be a great place, with fantastic people, but perhaps there was just something wrong with our karma. At least my stress over the corpse was swiftly fading. It seemed doubtful now that any murderers might be interested in me at all. I felt like I was guilty of an exaggerated evaluation of my importance in the whole business. *If I left them well alone*, I reasoned, why *wouldn't they do the same?* But too much thinking irritates the brain cells, so I stopped dwelling on it. But now I started to worry about the twins back home instead.

The twins' mom had sent me a few bizarre texts, calling me her fluffy rabbit and reminding me about going to the cinema with her that evening. That was odd, bearing in mind that we didn't normally call each other by animal names and that I would hardly be able to make it from Ireland to Latvia to see a movie that same day. Yet asking her over the phone just who the fluffy bastard was somehow didn't appeal to me either. It seemed much better to discuss such matters face to face. So I counted the money and considered the pros and cons. *OK*, I decided. *If nothing came up before we reached Dublin, I'd go home to La*tvia. There had to be a way to earn a living there. There just had to be.

Nothing did come up before Dublin, or in Dublin itself. Maybe we should have stayed in the city for longer; maybe we should have made friends among the locals and waited for a fortuitous job advert on a lamp-post, but somehow we felt fed up with the whole thing. So there we sat once again, in dirty old Dublin, rolling up tobacco salvaged from cigarette butts we had found on the street. If you only have to buy the Rizla papers, smoking isn't that expensive. Less tasty, though.

We observed the pigeons making their busy rounds by the station. The trip had been interesting, and there was even a little money left from our farming adventure, never mind the London earnings. However, we could hardly call it a successful mission either. I had found out that the flight to Riga would be much cheaper from London than it would be from Dublin. Screw the mafia killers of Canning Town: I had spent enough time in the

British Isles for now and it was the time to go back and spend my time at home as never before.

We spent our last night together in London, before our bus to Riga left from Victoria coach station. It was a good excuse to enjoy the hospitality of the Ukrainians once more. We raised our beer cans at seeing each other again, without realising then that we would be reunited much sooner than we thought. Agris felt moved almost to tears after just a couple of super-size cans of Carling and surprised everyone with an untypically friendly gesture.

"Misha," he said, "thank you ever so much for your help and hospitality. I don't have money to buy beers for the whole house or anything like that, but I would still like to leave you something nice as a thanks. Look what I've got. Now at least I will have the feeling I have done something for you as well."

He dug into his rucksack and produced a typical lads' magazine – a bit dog-eared and lacking a cover, but crammed full of supersize boobs, both fake and natural. I was surprised I hadn't seen it before.

"I found it on the street only today," he explained as if reading my thoughts.

He probably thought that the magazine's relative freshness would increase its value in the eyes of the Ukrainians. It didn't look like a very new issue, however, and looked distinctly second-hand (though admittedly held by one hand only). The Ukrainians giggled, rolled the magazine in a discreet scroll shyly and stuffed the magazine in the top drawer of the kitchen table – a place that was neutral yet accessible to anyone who was interested. Then they dealt out another round of beer cans.

Chapter 7

Those who migrate in these days of cheap airlines like Ryanair and Easy Jet don't have a clue how demanding and full of suffering the initial path was for the pioneers. Only after having done a London-Brussels-Warszawa-Vilnius-Riga three-day trip can you fully appreciate the blessings of what a cheap airline can bring, despite being plagued by adverts and ugly cabin attendants en route. Of course, it is annoying when people who own a whole fleet of Boeings beg you to buy their lottery tickets through their not-so-well-paid personnel. *It would be more effective*, I think, *if they had a lottery for more leg space or a seat where nobody asks you to buy a deodorant.* But it is still better than thirty-six hours on a bus, pressed between an ice-cold window and a piping hot labourer who snores cheap pork sausage breath and sweats so intensively you can almost hear his pores opening under the pressure of the vapour.

When I say 'labourer' I'm obviously aware of the fact that most of these folks were not labourers back home. Not at all. Before life forced them to migrate, it was likely that they were part of the 'intelligentsia' – a teacher, a shop manager, a doctor perhaps. These guys told everybody they were going to England on a 'business trip'. The catch was that the shiny new suits they came back with to impress their mates and lure girls into prospective sexual liaisons were earned not through business in a *Financial Times* sense of the word. No, it was a combination of countless hours of underpaid toil and massive savings in the quality of everyday life that bought their wealth.

Their mates would be duly impressed, yet feel sure their buddies hadn't changed that much because they would still detect that same mixture of fear and suspicion that had been in their eyes before they took their 'business trip'. It is difficult to disguise such deep-seated unease. Very truly I tell you, me and my generation – you can send us to the Sorbonne or Oxbridge, if you want, yet our thinking cannot be changed. For ours has been the self-education you get in the academy of Soviet and Post-Soviet Life. Sadly, it has taught us lots of wrong things and painted our inner selves grey with suspicion and fear. At least then I didn't know better.

That's why our first reaction to any kind of human interaction tends to be on the level of 'what do you want from me?' or 'why me?' We inwardly cringe in fear when a ticket controller enters the carriage – and it doesn't matter whether we have the ticket or not. When we do our ridiculously expensive shopping on Oxford Street or in Chelsea to satisfy the thirst of our souls for the glamour of a happy life, the earnings of many weeks and the superhuman strain of it all are visible in the angry tiredness in our eyes. We become grey and wrinkled, both inside and out, from never-ending overtime and the gratification that's delayed until forever. We gather around barbecues on our rare days off, and even the outrageously pricey t-shirts can't take our focus off the dark rings under the eyes of overworked young girls. Let the sun shine and the neighbours behind our garden fence chat happily to a background of Calypso or whatever – we have our own sad songs to listen to, and only alcohol can dilute the greyness and hopelessness that seems to be encoded in the very core of our DNA.

The bus to Riga took two nights and a day altogether. I arrived at Riga bus station in the early afternoon, and the culture shock of returning home cooled off my body and soul, overheated by the bus journey. The area of the Central Market beside the station, peopled by pigeons and sellers of home-grown vegetables, was as grey as ever. If the freshly refurbished cafés here and there created an illusion of modernity for a brief moment, then the good ol' attitude of Riga's service staff pricked the bubble instantly.

If you want to experience some scary adrenaline rush on a tourism trip, the Baltic states can offer you the ticket ladies on our public transport system. With this being the lowest paid work around, such roles are traditionally taken by pensioners. Unfortunately, the job serves only to burn out everything in their already tiny, dried-up souls till all that's left is hatred and a deep conviction that everyone is a fare dodger. I once read in a biology book that microorganisms actually must find it very hard to live in water, be it a pond or a bath, since their miniscule size makes it difficult for them to overcome the density of the water as they go about their micro-business. Their mass is too small to cope well with the density of water, you see. In just the same way an Eastern European ticket lady with her ticket roll is fighting for survival when she wades through a crowded bus, keeping an eye on everybody and making sure they have all paid for their tickets. Like an amoeba propelling itself in a pond by the means of pseudopodia locomotion, the ticket lady fights through her day, again and again proving herself to be fit for survival, until total burnout. Both microbes and ticket ladies find life equally stressful. An amoeba has enemies everywhere – bugs, whole colonies of volvoxes, not to mention the odd slug determined to gulp her down on sight, or what have you. The ticket lady, on the other hand, has only got one enemy, but – oh, mercy! – *What* an enemy! His name is the Passenger, and he's the evillest of all bastards! Sly and sneaky, the Passenger boards public transport full of mischief, harbouring an evil plot behind his seemingly innocent face – to cheat on the ticket price, to dodge the fare, to step on the ticket lady's feet, to tell her off and maybe even splash some ketchup from a takeaway on her uniform while she isn't paying attention.

Squeezed on a crowded tram, I quaked to the rhythm of the rail joints and found myself thinking about Gnosticism. Have you heard of the idea that this world is created by Satan and is actually hell? If you have ended up here, it is because you have sinned before in some higher, more spiritual dimension and are condemned to live in a material body in a material world as a punishment. Without a doubt, empirical observations on Eastern European public transport fully support this hypothesis. What is not clear, however, is this: a) is this a punishment programme for the passengers, with them being punished via the ticket controllers, or b) are we, the passengers, cloned in millions, here to punish the ticket ladies? It's a somewhat depressing thought – mom and dad had sex only so I could play a tiny role in the grand scheme called 'Help Your Ticket Controller Get an Ulcer Effortlessly'.

Assuming about a thousand people pass through a bus or tram while a ticket lady is doing her shift, that's about a thousand people upset and angry when they get off, and they might go on to take it out on whoever else happens to be around. A hundred ticket ladies – a hundred thousand messed-up human beings. Looking at things this way, we can easily imagine how our public transport starts to emanate strong negative energy first thing in the morning, especially during the peak hours. About, say, an hour before the start of the working day and some two hours after it ends, negative energy oozes like some kind of greyish matter from the bus and tram stops towards offices, cafés and surgeries. There, it gets picked up and distributed further. On the way home, we charge ourselves with it again, and finally share it with our families at home. And so it goes on, day after day, until the poison is integrated in your soul and has stained even your bone marrow.

Or maybe there are aliens who devour this energy? In that case, we can deduce that they're having their breakfast between seven and nine in the morning and then dinner after five.

After this long diversion, let me tell you how it was when I returned home for the first time. A few family snapshots, as it were. As you have probably gathered by now, the tram was full. What you probably weren't expecting is that along with my two yelling children I found my neighbour and childhood best friend Herbie waiting for me at the flat. He was sitting in his undies at the kitchen table, poking some smoked fish for breakfast with a fork. I put down my bag of presents and we shook hands awkwardly.

There is a Russian folk poem that goes:

> *Папа едет в Ленинград,*
> *Мамин хахаль будет рад.*
> *Мамин хахаль - наш сосед,*
> *Папа купит мне мопед!*

For those who are not well versed in Russian poetry, the meaning can be translated something like this:

> *Daddy leaves for Leningrad*
> *Mommy's fucker will be glad.*
> *Mommy's fucker lives next door*
> *I'll get some presents, that's for sure!*

Poetry is such an emotional genre, and a lot gets lost in translation...

When I entered the bathroom, it made me think of George Harrison. Do you remember he had an album called *All Things Must Pass*? How true... There was another toothbrush instead of mine and a new stripy towel I hadn't seen before. It smelt of builder's armpits, so I deduced it belonged to Herbie.

My first thought was, if he took the pains to bring his own toothbrush across from his own flat, which was literally just behind the wall, then this must be a proper long-term relationship with a vision for future.

Indeed, there was a vision.

"Howdy," said the twins' mom when she returned from shopping. Then it all came out in a bit of a rush. "You know, I've been thinking about taking a part-time job and I've started looking for a nanny. Will you still have a job when you go back? Herbie is doing some log cabins in Baltezers[16] at the moment, but they haven't paid him for a few weeks now. Without your support, we wouldn't even be able to buy firewood."

All right then. So I was off the family list but for the function of providing financial support. The role of the activity leader for sexual and cultural events had been passed on to Herbie. I spent that night at my drummer's place, cuddling the cold emptiness of the floor, rolled up like a doughnut around a hole.

Everybody insisted we record a song, and so we did. It came out quite sad this time around.

Family drags aside, coming home after a long working trip can actually be fantastic. You have cash in your pocket, new clothes, a stylish mobile phone. There is so much satisfaction in calling all your mates and inviting them out for a drink – and being able to pay for everyone. A builder returns home from abroad as a sea explorer from an expedition to a land of spices and elephants. We drink ourselves nearly dead and do other cool things. Some of us hire the best sluts in town; others upgrade the furniture in granny's house. The point is – are, for there's more than one – you've got more cash than you ever had before, the prices are low, and you have lots and lots of suffering behind you that you want to forget. We believe we deserve a break.

---

[16] A rich suburb of Riga.

Demanding wives and girlfriends, parents, and children who have been phoning constantly, emotionally blackmailing us to return, usually calm down after the first financially successful visit back home. Next time, not only do they not object, they may even force us to go again – and even come with us.

But never, ever, will they get to know the whole deal of what we, the pioneers, went through – the stressful queues at passport control; the interviews with immigration officers that led some to faint a half an hour before the interview even started; getting up at four in the morning to be able to cross town to work before the rush hour; the loneliness; the desperation; the sexual deprivation, when spermotoxicosis blinds your eyes and eliminates your ability to distinguish between young and old, beautiful and ugly – when any object, be it moving or static, if it even remotely reminds you of a woman, creates in your soul the strident squeak of a saw's teeth rasping across a nail. And given enough time, *everything* reminds you of women.

Come on, Foreignerski, I hear you saying, it can't be that bad. Some people have even met their wives and husbands on such trips. I agree. But not everyone is good at blending in, I'm afraid, and that leaves them in the empty shell category. I've got friends who follow the same strategy every year: nine months' non-stop work, seven days a week, and then three months at home in a black hole of alcoholic memory loss. When I say three months, I mean ninety days straight. On day ninety-one they wake up, wash their sore heads with cold water, have a quick hair of the dog and then borrow some cash for a single ticket back to the land of milk and honey, where jobs are plenty and profits waiting.

These types are not usually very keen on learning the lingo. I know a Polish dude who, during nine and a half years in London, only learned two phrases in English – actually, I suspect he thinks these are two words – disvan (this one) and katit (cut it). When pronouncing the second one of these, he usually amplifies the verbal signal by means of visual info, symbolically placing the index finger of one hand over the index finger of the other and making a cutting move. These two expressions have allowed him to establish a sufficient lifestyle, to deal with the transport system, work, shopping and any other social transaction that might include someone else apart from himself.

In the course of those nine and a half years, he has been back to Poland only three times, but doesn't remember any one of those visits: the first bottle got opened in Victoria coach station and when the last one was finished, he found himself on the bus going back to England. There is suggestive evidence, one might say, that all three vocational trips were highly successful and socially dynamic.

Now, before any UKIP member says 'Aha!' may I please point out the well-known and sad truth that native English speakers very rarely know even one word of any other language, which makes this Polish dude look pretty good against in the context of such a mono-linguistic background. What makes English the most widely spoken language in the world is not the population of Albion, or even Freedonia (aka the US), but us – the non-native speakers.

But let's get back to frittering away money. Some folks have a somewhat broader understanding of what entertainment means. You can, for instance, hire a boat on the River Daugava just for you and a girl you met that day for the first time. Or you can order a minicab and pretend to be a foreigner, speaking only in English with the poor driver (in post-Soviet countries, they are almost guaranteed to be bilingual, yet none of the languages they speak sounds even remotely like English). A refinement of this is to keep changing your mind about where you want to go till the driver goes nuts and begs you to leave. If there are two of you, you can play the game known as 'the mobile phone'. The rules are simple: in the hallway of some big building like a hotel, both players collapse on the ground, cuss loudly in English, and slide one or two brand new and very expensive phones across the floor between them in imitation of ice hockey. Since no one knows that in England mobiles come for free if you take them on a contract and that if you make a small monthly payment, you get a new phone when the old one gets lost (or is resold, let's be fair about it), people are seriously impressed by that one and think you must be foreigners.

Then there is the option of investing your hard-earned money in business. Those capable of setting up a business in England can summon their countrymen to an English *stroika* and pay them a Latvian salary in an English environment. Often these entrepreneurs earn decent money even by English standards, and they are loved by everybody. The key to their success is actually very simple. As explained before, as workers in England are employed mostly on a daily basis, not on price, you need to a) pay as little as possible per hour, and b) offer the builders lots of hours. Thus, if there is enough to do, the customer is happy about the amount of the work done and the workers about the salary they get for a fourteen-hour working day, leaving the entrepreneur to rake in the profit. If the workers are not good with the lingo and therefore can't operate websites such as eBay properly, the entrepreneur buys the electronic gadgets, motorbikes or whatever else their employees' passionate little hearts might desire, then resell them to the employees for the whole of the money they just received in their salary. Ta-da! The entrepreneur's expenses have now been reduced to close to zero. Perpetuum mobile.

Finally, if none of that seems flashy and impressive enough, you can simply walk up to a cash machine, withdraw your cash and toss it up into the air and watch it fall like rain. Been there, done that.

Naturally, not everyone in the motherland appreciates it when we behave like that. Most people feel some call for a counter-reaction, and if you buy them enough drinks, at some point they will start to accuse you of being a traitor and a deserter, someone who holds money above important things like national pride, and so on. Excuse me, money *is* important. All those loans and mortgages and the child support must be paid, and there is no way of paying them within the East European economy as it stands now. There are quite a few people who take a mortgage in Latvia and then pay it back from a salary earned abroad. Besides, when we left the country, those who stayed got more work to do, and less competition. In my personal case, it also turned out that I was indirectly responsible for more than my immediate family's well-being. After all, Herbie was living with the twins and their mom and if I withdrew my financial support he would find himself in the same situation I was in when I left. If I did withdraw it, though, he might take it out on my family, and I didn't want that to happen.

I had so much money that for the first month it seemed impossible I would ever spend it all. Just imagine: you take some two-hundred lats (that's Latvian money) off your card, then next day you stick it in the cash machine again, and wow! – There's still lots of money on it. So I drunk my drinks, bought my dream laptop, met my kids every other day and got a job with a traditional Latvian midget salary. But still... deep inside, I missed London's busy streets. Every now and then I would dream about the Thames and the Strand, the funny domes of the Royal Albert Hall and the Docklands skyscrapers. I know, some people reckon London is a rough and rude place. My answer to that is, you haven't been to Eastern Europe, mate.

So when Armand called one day and invited me to work in a *stroika* in Baker Street, not far from Regent's Park, I was ready to go. Regent's Park is one of my favourite places in London. Even a corpse in a concrete slab didn't scare me off anymore, even though I kept checking the BBC from time to time. There had been no mention of it in the news, so maybe I had just dreamt it all up. I didn't know the answer. I packed my bag, said farewell to colleagues and bought a ticket with all the money I had left. A single ticket.

I tried to talk to the twins' mom, and save my family – but the truth is she had nothing to say to me, just kept that grin on her face and sighed once in a while. All my variations on the theme 'How could you...?' were answered by a simple 'I don't know, it just sorta happened.' The eternal enigma of human interactional dynamics never got solved. At least not this time around.

Funny old chap, my mate Herbie. When they first met, they couldn't stand the sight of each other, and I had had to explain to her again and again that he was a cool guy, even though a roofer by occupation. His sense of humour was too weird for most girls, at least until they got used to it. As a true son of his generation, he knew his way around Latvian underground music. We had some wicked times in our youth, and for the most part 'to beer or not to beer' never was a question. Our sorts were usually the cheapest, but we pretended it was stylish to drink shitty lager. If we got a good job, we would go large and spend money on some brownish stuff, like brandy, and usually mixed it with coke. I remember how we used to piss off my wife-to-be, sitting in the kitchen with a bottle of brandy and talking about the eternal topics of human existence.

'What's the shittiest animal in the world?' Herbie would ask with an all-knowing smirk, and wave a ketchup-soaked piece of pork sausage in the air on his fork. And then he would declare loudly: 'The Australian Pooparoo!'

The funniest thing, though, is that they split up after only a year and now Herbie lives and works in Lincolnshire, in a tiny village with some five-hundred inhabitants.

Chapter 8

It felt like the whole of London town had been waiting for me. The Krasko brothers had just migrated back to Ukraine – they had earned enough, they said in their e-mail, so now it was time to invest their money in business back home. So the good old builders' den in Leyton all of a sudden had two rooms available, and my return was a blessing from heaven to everyone else that lived there. Regent's Park was blooming and full of sporty chicks fleeing from imagined chicken fat in their thighs, scarlet faces framed by the arcs of their earphones. Blokes, with beer cans in hand, marvelled at them running past, while pretending not to be at all interested in the up 'n' down movement of their breasts. The fountains spat frothy water from their adorned spouts, squirrels competed with ants for the contents of the rubbish bins, and generally, there was a feeling of chilling out and relaxation in the air. I absolutely loved it.

One of the first things I did upon my return was to visit the Sherlock Holmes Museum. The real Baker Street house isn't even one fifth as nice as the cosy little building in Riga Old Town, where in the Russian film my heroes Holmes and Watson – Vasily Livanov and Vitaly Solomin – lived. Oh, well, eventually our childhood dreams must lose out to reality. But I still enjoyed the look of the stylish fireplace and the initials of the queen shot into the wall with revolver bullets. Guess what – the place where I had my next job was just a few doors down. 'Twas a place where my sweat, blood and tears – never mind other bodily liquids we proletarians tend to shed more often that everyone else – were to earn me a new experience, which lifted me up to the level of a professional chippie.

Let's talk about professionalism, shall we? It is good to be a professional and to have a crystal clear understanding of what the heck you are doing, in the dust and stench, sweaty, red-faced, and stuck under a condensation-coated waste pipe that contains the freshly departed lunch of your colleague. Your slippery palm clasps your cordless drill, its tiny motor snarling with a desperate enthusiasm while you fight your battle with a rusty screw that seems to be glued in the floor joist with superglue. A floor above, a plasterer with a Bluetooth in his ear is arguing violently with his wife in Polish, and occasionally wet plaster and milky water mixed with diluted PVA splashes in your face through gaps between the old floorboards. With every turn of the screw bit, the screw loses a bit more of the cross-shaped groove on its head; then the drill squeals frantically and you know it is actually you who is screwed now because there will be at least half an hour of chiselling to get the bloody thing out – and you'll consider yourself lucky if you don't beat your hands senseless with the hammer in the process.

Now, this is exactly where professionalism matters. You see, a professional is a man who is able to describe the situation succinctly, yet expressively and meaningfully. It doesn't matter whether you are addressing the screw, the plasterer upstairs, the dying battery of your overworked cordless or the electrician who just sent the crap in the waste pipe so close to your face – a true builder will grasp the heart of the matter not only graciously and with jaw-dropping imagination, but also while keeping up the speed of his working performance. For instance muttering, 'Oh, you eyelet in the bull's arse; I hope somebody jizzes over your snout too!' under your breath to the plasterer as you wipe bits of Multi-finish out of your eye and twist the chisel at a different angle to broaden the hole around the screw head and then catch it with the hammer's claw. Or: 'What poisonous runs these sparks have sometimes', while keeping your hold on the drill when there is no way to avoid the drop of shiny, limpid condensation as it detaches itself from the surface of the cast iron wastepipe right above your forehead.

And you carry on chiselling, as graciously as you can in such a position. When you have widened the hole enough, you press the drill against the screw, wedge it with the claw hammer in your other hand, and attempt to apply to it some desperate push-me-pull-you movement. If you're lucky and no one upstairs stumbles upon a pile of rubbish, sending little streams of dust into your eyeballs; if you're lucky and it is possible to bend your helmeted head back far enough to gather the sweat in a pool at the back of the helmet and keep it out of your peepers; and finally, if you're truly lucky and the damned screw squeals and starts to twist itself out, the genuine professional does not cuss, but simply announces the good news, by saying, for example: 'Yesss, baby!'

A true professional applies maledictions at the right place and at the right time. It is important to understand, that in a *stroika*, coprolaliacan be an important source of additional energy. Inside the builder's brain, overheated not just by the helmet but also by the routine problems (unpaid bills, hangover, and etcetera) that eat his grey matter away like an annoying bunch of worms, high-quality heartfelt swearing releases a flood of happiness hormones. The poetic and rebellious power of raw, vulgar expletives offers an emotional discharge as well as the chance to express one's linguistic imagination and relieve the boredom of much building work. People misunderstand when they assume there is no difference between a builder and someone with Tourette's syndrome. Yet there is. Once an elderly lady from next door came down to our site to complain about the language and asked for the general manager, who happened to be a Pole with a particularly strong inclination to swear. She tried to express her protest as politely as she could, in the best Oxbridge-trained Received Pronunciation. Why on earth, she inquired, did we have to use so many foul words? She had a nosy little three-year-old granddaughter, who repeated what she overheard coming from next door. And is Mr Kurwa[17] our boss, she asked, since we mention him so often. If so, she would like to discuss the issue with this gentleman.

"Darlying," our manager began in reply, "let me show you something." He gallantly opened an inner door that led into a corridor dangerously stacked to the ceiling with plasterboard, floorboards, chipboard, master boards and the board of directors, who were represented by a tattooed, ginger-bearded Australian foreman and a little Indian guy with gold-rimmed glasses and a very dirty suit. Both men were wearing ties and holding dusty

---

[17] *Kurwa*, in Polish, means 'slut'. It is one of the favourite expletives used in Eastern Europe outside the former Soviet bloc, where we use a different term.

cups of tea in their hand, while discussing impatiently 'the fucking drawings of a cunt of an architect'. The manager coughed and closed the door.

"Darlying," he repeated. That's right, with that soft 'ly' sound, so characteristic of Polish language. "zisiz a fucking builyding site, so vat do you vant?"

The lady had nothing to say to that. There were no more protests, and we kept on building Britain the same way we did before.

Conclusion: a true professional not only knows what he is doing; he also can see his work within a particular theoretical framework and explain to a non-professional, understandably, how less obvious aspects fit into it.

The above examples will allow the reader to infer, logically, that my next trip to London was to be much more focused on getting some education in my trade, less on messing around. I actually began to gain real experience in skilled construction work. My Polish vocabulary grew exponentially alongside the skills I acquired. Countrymen of Stanislaw Lem and Nicolaus Copernicus comprised an ethnic majority on our site, where I was taken on as a chippie. They let me do the joists and later cover them with floorboards from the top and plasterboard from below, thus creating floors and ceilings. No doubt I found it all new and interesting, yet years later, if I've had a dodgy kebab before going to sleep and insomnia kicks in, I still toss and turn worrying about those joists and the fact that someone might have their heavy furniture, TV, maybe even a grand piano, resting on them now. Little do they know that they are relying upon planking laid by a complete idiot.

I hear you saying: if you can't change it, don't worry about it. Damn right. And even if the first rooms I worked on were probably quite dodgy, my next ones were much better. I swear I did my best, but I did – do – feel responsible.

The advances I made in my professional life at this time were largely made possible by the aforementioned site manager. He was a Pole with a strong love of beer, football, and small, skinny women. If a nice-looking female passed our site he would wolf-whistle in excitement. For a man pushing his sixties, his sexual drive was enviable. At the same time, the level of his sensitivity towards the feelings of others was so low that he wouldn't have any qualms about discussing the risks of childbirth or embryonic pathology with a pregnant woman or, indeed, sharing his scathing opinions about the hapless efforts of a novice builder like me.

"*Wilhelm, jesteś dupa nie budowlaniec,*" he declared after the first couple of hours I spent under his leadership.

I goggled back at him. *Did he just call me an arse of a builder?*

"I'll keep you as a carpenter, but you will have to learn. Use your brain as much as you can, and don't annoy me too often with questions. Since you understand shit all, I'll pay you a hundred quid a day and teach you all I know. But you will have to be patient."

Janusz definitely wasn't very patient himself. You could tell his whereabouts by simply standing still for a short while and listening for bilingual cursing. He emanated swearing as the sun radiates light, enriching the day with such linguistic pearls as 'bloody kurwa fuck' and 'builder's dupa[18]'. He also provided me with a few moments of cultural and professional revelation, however. It was with Janusz and our multinational gang of chippies that I first went to a real British pub, for instance. The pub in question was The Volunteer at 245–247 Baker Street. We went there every Friday and it was during these visits that I came to realise why racism is such total bullshit. No colour provides safety from suffering on the great *stroika* of mad capitalism; but the liquid amber of a cold pint washes all bitterness away. For beer is the same colour for everybody, and its relaxing and unifying properties count for a lot after you have been killing yourself to live[19] for five days straight.

It was at the pub that Janusz would let his philosophical side show through.

"Have a look around;" he said. "Observe the level of the floor. Now the level of the window sills. Pay attention to the joints. Is anything at all straight and level in this place? It isn't. Because that's something the Brits never pay attention to. As long as the thing is somehow wacked on at least roughly where

---

[18] Arse.(Polish)

[19] Not my quote, unfortunately. It's Black Sabbath, in case you didn't know.

it is supposed to be, they're happy. Try to present such a job in Poland and you would lose your customers. But not here."

Kevin, one of the English plumbers, who had accidentally come along, understandably felt insulted. "How many immigrants had relevant qualifications when they came to this country?" He asked venomously. "How many of them arrived knowing what to do? Look at Greg," he went on, "he's Polish and pretends to be a bricklayer, yet he clearly has very little understanding of what he does. It takes him ages to build a partition because he's doing it for the first time." He tries his best, Kevin admitted – the security man had told him that Greg turned up at work two hours before everybody else, otherwise he wouldn't be able to keep up with the more professional brickies. But what good could he do for Britain?

I hid my nose in my glass and pretended to be interested in the patterns of froth in it. I knew Greg reasonably well – we had been chatting in the canteen and I had learned new words from him in both Polish and English. The thing with Greg was, he used to be a medical doctor in Poland and before becoming a bricklayer in the UK, had been lecturing at a university. It was hardly a promising start for a career in construction, I had to admit. It showed, however, how vulnerable even well-educated immigrants are to criticism.

But Janusz just swept these considerations away with a wave of his majestic hand.

"Greg will learn," he said simply. "But I don't have to. I pay my taxes and I give jobs to others. I have twelve chippies working for me in three sites across London. I am building a carpenter's workshop next year. Have you ever seen me doing a job that was not perfect?"

Kev wasn't going to give up easily.

"Your work is fine," he admitted, "but did you have any qualifications when you came to this country?"

"I did," Janusz said. "At the age of fourteen, I won a bronze medal in a chess tournament for young players in Warsaw. Now, I work ten hours a day, six days a week. I haven't been on holiday for six years, and last year I paid enough in taxes to buy a second-hand Bentley. God willing, next year my tax will be worth a new one. How often do you go on holiday?"

"That's not the point," Kev insisted.

And on and on they went. Immigrants this, British that. You know, the hard talk.

At one point Kevin went for a leak, and Janusz bought a round.

"Just don't tell him," he said, while placing glasses in front of each of us, "I have lived in this country for fourteen years now, and with every year I become more like the Brits. And with every year, I enjoy my becoming British more and more. But I don't want them to know that. I like to keep my distance."

To those people who say, 'This is London – everybody is out for himself so don't expect any help from anybody' I would like to point out that London, along with the rest of the world, is full to the brim with brilliant, helpful folks. If there were no such people, this book would never have been written. Janusz is a great guy, a great professional chippie, and thanks to him I have not only earned some money but also learned a trade. Now I am actually able to do something decent with my hands! *Dziękuję bardzo pana.*[20]

An interesting, even fatal, twist in my life happened in the business of flat-sharing. As I mentioned before, upon my return to London I settled down with the Ukrainians again, in Leyton. Since there was one more room still available, we were on the lookout for a new flatmate and it was me who found one. It was Rahima, the Pakistani girl Agris and I had met in Ireland not so long ago. She arrived out of the blue, with her hair all over the place and two massive bags on wheels, yet still with all her charms intact.

Rahima broke into my life just like that. I had gone out to send some money back home from the Money Gram office by Victoria Station and was heading towards the Underground when Rahima stormed out of the main Overground station building and literally crashed into me by the stairs that lead down to the tube.

I couldn't help noticing that her crash buffering assets were as lovely as ever. Rahima had just arrived in London and was as angry as a swarm of crazed bees. She had been let down by a friend of hers who had offered to put her up. At the last minute, even as Rahima's train had been rolling into Victoria, the friend

---

[20] Thank you very much, sir. *(Polish)*

82

had phoned to cancel the plan. On top of that, Rahima rushed to add, she had just ditched Antonio because he was too jealous. Nice intro.

There was a brief moment of awkward silence after that. I gathered up the courage to invite her for a drink, to help her look for a solution. We hit a pub near the park and found a place in the corner, hiding ourselves behind her massive travel bags. I ordered some Kronenbourgs. It was my payday; I just had sent a round sum off to Latvia and felt that my karma was OK for now. I could afford to buy a cool pint for a hot chick.

And hot she was. From the conversation that followed, it sounded like Antonio had not only pissed her off but also starved her sexually – either that or they had recently been having problems achieving orgasmic union. Almost as soon as we had sat ourselves down at the dark mahogany, varnished table adorned with spilt beer and taken our first sip from our glasses, she dived deep to the root of her problems. I felt a bit weird, yet what could I say? You can't tell someone to shut up because they are torturing you with lust. Especially when you haven't had sex with anyone but yourself for ages.

"I need somewhere to live," she confided briskly. "Also, I need to stuff my fanny – oh God, Antonio – what a wanker. He pisses me off."

I soon discovered that for Rahima just about everything 'pisses me off'. It later turned out to be the diagnosis of her lifetime and the motto of her existence. Back then, I thought she was simply passing through a phase. Obviously, she had a lot of steam to let off, and she spent the next three hours illuminating intimate details of her sex life. Even though it all had come rather unexpectedly and my plan for the evening had been a quiet night in watching Eurovision or something similarly stupid, I tried to take it as a man and listened thoughtfully. She complained about Antonio over and over, stressing how narrow-minded he was and how old-fashioned he could be about letting her enjoy some freedom. That was why she had celebrated dropping him in Birmingham and getting her revenge by having a '3+2' orgy. Three girls and two boys, that is.

"You should have heard one of them bitches moanin' when I stuck my dildo in! Everybody says a woman can lick a woman out much better than a man. I hate to prick the bubble, but that's a myth. Now, dildo-ing, that's where the real skill shows itself. We can give it much better than any bloke. We feel the right angle, the tempo and the insertion depth way better than you selfish males. Men just poke away, thinking about themselves. What do they know of a woman's needs?"

A tattooed punk with rings in both eyebrows pulled his hood over his eyes, grabbed his pint and moved a few tables further away from us.

"Antonio always complained that my bum is too big, and wanted me to eat less. But you should have seen how eagerly those guys wanked about us girls, when the three of us got down on all fours in front of them! Fucking Antonio! He pisses me off, he really does!"

I scanned the room discreetly. London is a city of free and open minds, yet I felt a bit... strange.

We drank another pint of Kronenbourg, then some London Pride and John Smith Smooth. Towards the end of the conversation, it felt as if I was locked away in the wanking booth of a sex shop with both hands tied. The open-mindedness of this woman was simply killing me. I probably should have offered to help her have her revenge one more time; it would have been simple to organise a quickie in the pub lavatory or maybe take her home for a longer session. It dawned on me that we had an empty room at home and she had no other friends in London apart from the one that had let her down. After the fourth pint, the law of hospitality seemed to be the most logical law of the universe and I suggested she stay with us at least till she found something better.

"Are they all Russians there?" She asked a bit suspiciously. Well, yes and no, I told her, Eastern Europeans, but not Russians.

"That's what I meant. Good. I like living with Russ... Eastern Europeans. They always pay on time and wash the dishes after themselves. I hate living with the British – they never pay on time and then the electricity gets cut off."

We took off to the Victoria line. The charm of immigrant life lies partially in the simplicity of our communication and connectivity. Life is very hard sometimes and you often lack the contacts you need, so we tend to create friendships easier. Very often, with people coming and going, we find we only know one or two people the length and breadth of the country, so we have to make the best of the worst. Plus, we have no personal histories when we arrive, which gives us a massive advantage when starting our new lives.

Of course, you can't keep it like that forever. After a while, the ripples of your activities reach other people and overlap; you establish a reputation, and once again you have to learn to live with that reputation.

Rahima, who was from Ramsgate in Kent originally, was only just about to start building her reputation in London, and I was a lucky find for her – useful and even necessary. She was obviously encouraged by the fact that there was another woman in the house and that she would have a room all to herself.

We passed the journey chatting, most of it about Antonio and his irritating habits. By the time we got to Leyton, the effects of the beer were wearing off and a ray of clear consciousness broke through the colourful images of group orgies and so on that had filled my mind. Rahima must have experienced something similar, too, as she suddenly corrected her t- shirt where it had become too tight and informed me she had no intention of shagging me. She had told me a little about what was wrong in her life at the moment not because she wanted to do anything with me but just to get it off her enviable chest.

I had to promise her I would respect her untouchable status, even though the pressure inside me to seduce her was enormous. It seems that an aroused man will promise a woman absolutely anything – even that they will not have sex.

I tried to distance myself from my reproductive urges and instead consoled myself with the thought that the presence of another English speaker in the house would be very helpful in improving my language skills. Right.

That night, the lamp-posts on Lea Bridge Road seemed to glare like the lanterns of a red-light district. My dreams consisted of a mosaic of moaning sluts, vibrators and boobs. Complete marasmus orgasmus, as they would probably say in Pig Latin.

Anxious and unsatisfied, I examined the bedsheet next morning, but there were no signs of any penile discharge. Evidently I had grown too old for that. What a relief.

Chapter 9

Rahima was welcomed to our abode in an atmosphere of worshipful excitement and exaggerated Eastern European gallantry. The eyes of the lads lit up from inside, ignited by the hormonal injection as tends to happen when there has been no woman around for several months and then one unexpectedly appears – especially one so exotic, with a permanent genetically inherited tan set off by a couple of shiny piercings, her charming accent and her magnificent boobs seemingly about to burst out of her décolleté. It's a wonder really that nobody went bonkers over her right away.

Our female housemate Lillian was less enthusiastic, of course. Later she confessed she would normally have felt very jealous but over the last couple of weeks she had been shagging the head chef at the restaurant where she worked so she was fairly oblivious to the newcomer whose arrival threatened to overwhelm everybody else in the household. Besides, she was about to leave London anyway – the chef was a Frenchman, and his parents owned a house somewhere in the Alps. It would be silly for her to miss the opportunity, even though the chef was twice her age.

It feels relevant at this point to digress into some discussion of sex or, as some people in London call it, jigi-jigi. For starters, jigi-jigi doesn't happen very often, not to everyone anyway. I read somewhere that the eyes are the windows of the human soul and my observations prove it, at least when it comes to sex. If you look closely at your fellow passengers on the train during rush hour, especially the labourers, you soon learn to read the book of the soul as it manifests in their tired eyes. Quite a few of them are forever casting glances at the women passengers, whatever their age, colour and size, their stares loaded with adoration and despair mixed. Lots of construction workers and other labourers in the UK are foreigners, and most of them are at least theoretically tied to women and children back home. In any case, they usually lack the language skills, money and courage to build relationships with British girls. Wanking is not much of a solution – the more you do it, the more you need, and hence the more you despair.

The quiet desperation that comes with unsatisfied urges is best illustrated by a real-life situation that occurred concerning an illegal DVD vendor on our building site at Baker Street. Most DVD vendors I've seen are Chinese, and most have very rudimentary English with, say, just a couple of expressions such as: 'One DVD three pound, three DVD seven pound! This new film!'

At least twice a week our local Chinaman would turn up on the site and wander around during the tea break, with his produce wrapped up in a Tesco bag. He must have been a novice, for his pidgin was utterly incomprehensible. As many of them do, he wore a lousy and heavily worn canvas coat, the type our country folks were wearing during the Soviet times when cow-herding. His suit trousers, so old the knees were of a lighter colour than the rest of the trouser leg, were nevertheless clean and perfectly ironed. The hair at his temples was snowy white (must have been from crossing the border hiding in a refrigerator truck, I couldn't help myself thinking) and no matter how hard he tried the sounds of the strange language he was trying to speak never came out right.

He was approached by one of our plasterers, a young Indian lad.

"Hi, mate. Have you got any sexy films?"

The vendor stretched out his hand with some action movies.

"No, I want some dirty movies!"

The vendor pulled out a bunch of animated films, with *Shrek* on the top of the pile.

"No, no! I want some blue movies, porn, shaggin', you know?"

The Chinaman shook his head and produced another pack from behind his belt, the top cover featuring Bruce Willis, then nervously added something that was probably meant to be 'One DVD three pound, three DVDs seven pound.'

Jamaican Rob, who worked as a hod-carrier, a really massive bloke with a deep bass voice that boomed as low as a proper dub remix, put his fingers together in the internationally recognised gesture that all around the globe represents human intercourse:

"Jigi-jigi, mate!"

Oh yes, now our vendor caught the meaning! He produced a pack of discs that had been hidden behind his belt round the back, all with covers featuring naked tits and asses, and sighed in a voice so heartfelt and profoundly emotional that hushed even the noise of construction:

"Aah, jigi-jigi…"

The cultural and linguistic barriers came tumbling down and we felt as if spiritually holding hands for a moment. Here we were, at the edge of a construction pit torn in Mother Earth's flesh, in an artificial hell created by giant machines of insane capitalism, a valley of sorrow, an oppressive, brutal, money-churning limbo; and even though we came from all around the world, at that moment we reached out to each other in complete mutual understanding. In a brief moment of spiritual oneness, we realised we shared the same blood, the same sadness, the same trouble. And a trouble shared is a trouble halved.

Yet a sausage shared leaves you with a sausage halved, or only a half a sausage, that is. Without realising it, our vendor had hit upon a nice marketing trick. We all bought at least one copy of something.

I took a couple of action films, if you want to know. I told you, wanking does not help.

On this note, one of my mates had an interesting episode. One day, he decided to relax in the common room of his house by surfing the internet. He put the music on, got his beer out of the fridge and started to surf the *inappropriate* websites, if you know what I mean. All of a sudden his flatmates turned up, opened the door and came in. The poor geezer had to jump up and get his trousers closed up, and that's when the classic fault with the zipper occurred. Whatta bugger. Luckily, he was able to cover his embarrassment with his laptop and retreat to his room with dignity. Unfortunately, he had to quit cycling to work for the next couple of days, even though the job wasn't that far away and public transport in London is pricey.

Meanwhile, the dynamics of life in our household were evolving fast. Nansen hadn't paid his rent for six weeks, having had no luck finding a job. For ages, he had fed himself from the fridge shelf of the kind-hearted Krasko brothers but the repatriation of his sponsors forced him to make new arrangements. His initial plan, just to carry on as before without the Kraskos, fell through after Lillian complained in front of everybody else that Nansen had been eating the dumplings from her lunchbox. So, about a week or so after Rahima moved in, he tried to seduce her, failed, and then realised all he could do was man up and save on the rent money (which he didn't have anyway). The situation was saved when good old Armand found him a labourer's position in a *stroika* on the far northern outskirts of London. Nansen spent his first week's pay on a tent and some corned beef, and settled down in a park next to the site among the squirrels and birds. The job was literally on his doorstep and, most importantly, he had no rent to pay. Heaven on earth. Our Nansen had become an eco-tramp or, as he liked to call himself in French, a *clauchard*.

One thing he hadn't taken into account in calculating this perfect equation was the absence of easily accessible fresh running water, which was in direct ratio to the inevitability of getting mighty fragrant during the course of doing heavy construction work. On top of this, England is very well known to be a place where it rains on a frequent basis – and sometimes so fiercely that the natives have invented the scary expression 'horizontal rain' to describe it. This occurs when a downpour is driven horizontally by the wind so that the rain appears to be coming from the side, not from above. The tent, the sleeping bag and eventually Nansen himself were all soon being seriously challenged by the rainstorms, damp, and varied microorganisms of Epping Forest. All he could do by way of fighting back was to visit friends who owned showers and washing machines.

But we'll come back to that later. While Nansen was camping and getting closer to nature, our little house on Lea Bridge Road witnessed another plot development. Vlad, one of the Ukrainians we shared the flat with, a huge bloke somewhat akin to a gigantic baby with such big blue eyes that their childish stare was simply irritating – decided to be next to try to seduce Rahima.

Vlad's method was rather more sophisticated than Nansen's. His biggest difficulty was his English, the level of which was proportional to the amount of time he had spent studying it – that is, close to zero. His plan was also hampered by another obvious fact, that Rahima was not a girl to be won over cheaply. It would be an expensive business, or at least expensive from a kitchen porter's point of view, that being his job. Nansen had failed with Rahima (according to Vlad's theory) because he hadn't known how to blow her away with lots of attention, taking her out to fancy restaurants and movies, and plying her with fine wines and Ferrero Rochers before attempting the actual seduction. I recalled the Red Stripe Rahima had knocked back with us in Mullingar and pulled a face, but kept my mouth shut. In a way, he was right. Nansen might, indeed, have done better to adopt a more civilised approach. Don't get me wrong – sometimes it pays to be honest and straightforward about your feelings, but trying to lure a girl to bed by stripping naked in front of her and rest of the house, even after a litre of vodka has been shared, is a long shot, don't you think? And a passionate description of your desires in a language she does not understand is also less than likely to succeed – particularly if everybody else in the room is laughing their bollocks off because they *do* understand. They say it is possible to laugh a woman into bed, but the joke really has to be in a language she understands – and no one but native-born Latvians speak Latvian even in Ukraine, never mind the UK or Pakistan.

And so Vlad forged a plan that featured me in a big, I would even dare to say crucial, role. According to this plan, I had to find Vlad a job on my *stroika* in Baker Street, where he could master both the English language and the carpenter's trade. His improved language skills would allow him to approach his beloved in a manner she understood, while the improved salary he earned with his trade skills would give him the financial means to impress her. In return, he promised to stay grateful to me to the end of his days. He would also take me to the pub at his expense.

The casual observer might detect a few vulnerable points in this plan. Vlad, for instance, had never so much as touched a hammer in his life. But let's not forget, this is London and hey, the whole of life is just a freaky poker game where kismet often prefers to deal different crap instead of fours and royals. And when you are an Eastern European just trying to survive, your best approach is often to play for high stakes, even if kismet takes a piss and deals you chess pieces instead of cards in a pool tournament and according to backgammon rules. That's how adaptive you have to be. To elaborate the point, I could also mention that in reality kismet almost never looks our way at all. When we show somebody our casino chips, they turn out to be photocopied, dog-eared, with fatty stains, won in the Russian national game *gorodki*, and rejectable by most standards.

Anyway... Vlad had asked for help, and I didn't really see any reason to refuse him. The site seemed to expand every day, and I knew there were lots of jobs to do. I spoke to the site manager. He did need labourers, and we agreed that Vlad would also be allowed to work with me when possible, to pick up some chippentry tricks. Not that I knew much myself – I didn't have much more than the tools and my ambitions, and was still learning myself.

To sum up, generally speaking, overall, if you *really* thought about it, there were no obstacles to Vlad becoming the same as me.

Or were there? Since I had been employed by an agency for a quite a while now, I had forgotten that not everybody can get it the easy way, like me.

Vlad was Vlad to me and to his mum, when he phoned back home. On the site, though, our Vlad magically transformed into Audis Boozerkevicus. This magical change was a consequence of the feeble attempts of the United Kingdom to keep Ukrainians, Russians and other hungry folks away from their bulging lunchbox. Citizens of the Baltic states are currently leaders in this race for survival; at the moment we are allowed to work legally in most European countries, while those in countries further to the east stand holding onto the barbed wire fences, salivating. Those who lack the courage, that is. The brave hearts like Vlad sneak into Lotusland on tourist or student visas and then a) get married to somebody with the right citizenship (standard market price three-thousand pounds); b) buy a Latvian or Lithuanian passport (cheaper, but illegal); or c) simply don't give a crap and just do their best, hoping that their lack of language skills will prevent any unfortunate incidents. Vlad had chosen b). He had bought a Lithuanian passport in the name Audis Boozerkevicusand paid for it a sum which he refused to make known to the wider public.

As it turned out, it was not easy to be a Boozerkevicus. For starters, Vlad could not spell his new name to the site manager – and he found it difficult to memorise the exotic sounds of the language. At the same time, he was scared to show the passport to the manager since the photo wasn't *exactly* like him. It wasn't that the original Boozerkevicus was ugly or anything – our Vlad had simply saved some pounds and bought only the passport, without changing the photo. On the day of purchase, he had convinced himself that he and the original owner looked so similar they could have been twins. However, when a real-life situation turned up in which the passport was to be used, he started to falter and wished he had paid the extra to get his own photo inserted in the thing. After all, for gluing in a new photograph, Lithuanian forgers only charged fifty quid. I had to come to the rescue and helped Vlad out with the spelling of his new name. Fortunately, Latvian and Lithuanian are related languages.

By the way, in case you are wondering, Latvian and Lithuanian might be related but they are nothing like Russian. And no, we are *not* Russians, even those of us who can speak the language really well. If you are born in a country like India, say, it's most likely you speak at least some English, as India used to be an English colony – but that does not make you an English person, right? My generation, and those who are older can speak Russian because we had to learn it while living in the USSR. The younger generation doesn't understand Russian at all. That's why communications between ex-Soviet nations nowadays are mostly in English. Yet me and my Eastern European buddies always converse in Russian, since it is the lingua franca of our childhood and youth.

Eventually, the Baker Street adventure turned out to be very stressful and panicky for Vlad. As soon as he got out of the manager's office, he stumbled upon an even more threatening challenge. That very same day a whole gang of Lithuanian chippies was hired. When he met up with the guys, the poor lad had to introduce himself as Audis – a distinctively Lithuanian name. Vlad's vocabulary in Lithuanian was about twice as big as his vocabulary in English – I had taught him all I knew myself, i.e., 'labas dienas[21]' and 'gerai[22]'. It was hardly sufficient to hold a conversation. The dialogue that followed went roughly like this:

'Labas, is kuro miesto esi?'[23]
"Eh?"
"What's your name?"
"Audis."
"Where are you from?"
"Eh?"
"Ты откуда?"[24]
"ИзМосквы."[25]

This was followed by an impromptu improvisation in an attempt to explain why someone called Audis Boozerkevicus didn't understand a word of Lithuanian. According to this new-born legend, Audis's mother was a Russian from Moscow, and he had spent most of his life there. *If so*, I thought to myself, *why do you speak Russian with such a terrible Ukrainian accent?* Incidentally, Vlad later told me he had never been to Moscow. It was simply the first place that came to mind.

From now on, as soon as the Lithuanians appeared on the horizon, Vlad jerked desperately and tried to disappear – sometimes with a rubbish bag over his shoulder, sometimes with a piece of chipboard or plasterboard in his hands, and inevitably ended up getting stuck in the doors, tangled up in power cables and so on. When the site manager appeared to distribute duties each morning, Vlad lost the baby pink in his cheeks and only got it back on when he was commanded to work with mostly Jamaican bricklayers or the plumbing team, which was one-hundred per cent English. He was even scared of being with me because, as a chippie, I was often put to work alongside the Lithuanian gang.

---

[21] Hello.(Lithuanian)
[22] Good.(Lithuanian)
[23] Hello, which city are you from? *(Lithuanian)*
[24] Where are you from? (Russian)
[25] From Moscow.(Russian)

Our evening conversations were often spoiled by his paranoia about the Lithuanians, as though he feared they were stalking him.

"Why on earth were they asking where I'm from? Why are they so interested?"

"Because they heard your Lithuanian name. So they assumed you were Lithuanian as well."

"OK, OK, but why did they ask for my name? I wouldn't have had to say it aloud, if not for them asking!"

Another problem with the Audis name was Vlad's inability to react to it instantly when it was called. Sometimes he received clear instructions to do this or that, but did nothing beyond glancing expectantly at somebody next to him and obviously wondering to himself how it could be that this Englishman / Latvian / Jamaican / Indian / Ukrainian tick appropriately came to have a Lithuanian name. So now we had a man in our *stroika* who on one hand boiled with energy and was happy to do anything asked of him, like he was a puppy being taken for a walk, but on the other hand seized up whenever a chippie appeared and was apparently haunted by the fear that they were stalking him. A couple of times Vlad almost headed for the hills when he saw a Lithuanian exiting the office door. In addition to all this, the reality of everyday working life was opening his eyes to the fact that a few days or even weeks wouldn't be sufficient to make him into a master builder. Yet at the end of his dark tunnel, there shone a golden cup of victory, held by the manicured palms of a goddess with massive boobs.

What, with Vlad's jumpy presence about the place, I now found that instead of a single leisurely can of beer after work I had to finish one off quickly just to become able to relax enough for the proper enjoyment of a second one. Vlad meanwhile would continue to buzz around me like a blue-arsed fly, ensuring I really needed that double dose.

"I saw one of them entering the manager's office today. Just tell me, for heaven's sake, why do these Lithuanians need to go in there? Do you think they talk about me?" He repeated the question again and again. "The site manager looked at me really strangely this afternoon. I think they've found out!"

I sat back on our dodgy sofa and tried to unwind my senses while staring at a dark spot of fungi growth on the ceiling. *It must be the bathroom right above me*, I thought; *could be a leak from the bath*. All our furniture had been found on the street, since furnished rooms cost more, and nobody was going to spend any money on chairs or tables – too expensive. The washing-machine leaked and some of the chairs were dangerous to sit on.

Of course, I could understand where Vlad was coming from. If somebody took a closer look at his passport and posed a couple of tricky questions, he would be on his way back to Vinnytsia at the expense of Her Majesty. On the other hand, every other Ukrainian I knew was here on a student's visa (there were quite a few 'colleges' at the time that didn't offer English as such, just visa extensions for a modest fee) and my own papers were a photocopied marvel of a forgery, a criss-cross between my own and Armand's passports that I had made myself, to save money. There were rumours at the time that citizens of new EU states would be able to get into Lotusland without any special visas pretty soon, so I could simply wait until the gates opened and allowed me to dip into the milk and honey legally. The Ukrainians had no such hope, and Vlad had grounds to freak out about the risk of being exposed.

Yet there is a line to be drawn between a worry and uncontrolled panic. I took a big gulp of beer and turned towards the fake Boozerkevicus.

"I just talked this over with the site manager today. I'm afraid I have bad news for you."

Vlad reached for a chair and lowered his arse slowly onto it, eyes fixed on me.

"The Lithuanians have called the British secret service in. The Jamaican brickies are actually just pretending to be working on the *stroika*; in fact, they are spying for the British government."

Vlad swallowed heavily and his face acquired a pained 'I fucking knew it!' expression. Vlad had distrusted the Jamaicans from day one.

"I don't really know how they managed it," I went on, "but somehow these spies got their hands on samples of your blood and urine. They have been told by the laboratory that you have no Lithuanian DNA and now you are considered to be very suspicious."

I took another sip of beer and enjoyed the look of fear on Vlad's face as it ran across his features like ripples in water after someone's thrown a brick in.

"The manager says you should either turn up in the office first thing in the morning to give urine and blood samples in his presence, so he can double-check, *or*, you can go to the court and piss in the courtroom. In any case, the mobile analyst brigade will be present, as it is the normal procedure when there are foreigners with suspicious passports involved. All the expenses, of course, must be paid for by you. On top of that, if the double-check doesn't find any Lithuanian DNA in your piss and blood, you will have to pay a fine and return all your wages to the employer. The good news though is that deportation is practically free – meaning you'll only have to return the money for deportation if your income is above fifteen-thousand British pounds a year, and you won't earn that much in Ukraine. So – easy, mate."

We sat in silence for a while. The boiler in the kitchen clicked, and something reverberated in the water pipes. I squashed the empty can in my hand, attempted a throw into the Tesco bag hanging from the kitchen door handle, missed and reached lazily for another one.

Vlad's green face slowly returned to its regular pink hue.

"You're pulling my leg, aren't you? Are you?"

Suddenly, I felt sorry for him. I stretched, yawned and closed my eyes.

"Of course I am, Vlad. Grab a bevvy and chill out."

Chapter 10

Despite Vlad being so scared, I got along with the Lithuanians pretty well. All of them were obsessed with God and tried to preach during the tea break, but that actually made quite a nice change; otherwise we always read the newspapers.

The true builder usually reads a tabloid during his break. As a builder myself, I have made several observations over the years about the reaction of my body and soul to screws, saws, sweaty socks and steel-toe boots, and have come up with a theory. It goes like this. Everybody knows what a callus is, right? Lazy folks develop calluses on their hands during their rare sessions of spring cleaning, whereas a builder develops them constantly and in many places simultaneously: on his palms, his heels and in his brain. The latter develop as a consequence of constant physical tiredness and stress. When you get pissed off by a plasterboard construction that refuses to level out or your employer barks madly about you being too slow, only a pint and a third page girl can rescue you. Screw Margaret Atwood – you are reading to relax, not to imbue your soul with the *Weltschmertz*. Let's get real: in the real world, humans suffer real pain and they don't need an imaginary one to add to it. Celebrity gossip can have a healing effect sometimes.

We usually read *The Sun* or *Adult Sport*. The latter is more focused on celebrity arses and upskirts, as the first part of the name suggests. *The Sun*, on the other hand, used to be my favourite for learning English while I was in the initial stages of linguistic development. Its beauty lies in its patient repetition of the same thing over and over, until even the dumbest foreigner is able to get it. Every sentence is treated as a separate paragraph, to ease the intake of information, and the letters are fairly big, too. In terms of grammar, sentences are unsophisticated, to say the least, and tend to be very short, to avoid punctuation that could otherwise burn out the reader's brain if used in overwhelming numbers. In case you don't get the meaning of the heading, there is the gist of the message in the subheading, in bold letters, basically paraphrasing the heading; in other words, it's an abstract of what is to follow. Then there is the main body of text in several sentence-paragraphs, delivered in a snap, snap, snap style. To non-Brits, every article looks something like this:

Harry's
cocaine sniffing
Somebody close to the
Royal family has leaked
out that Harry's sniffed
cocaine!

The Editor has heard that Prince Harry uses drugs.

This time, it's cocaine.

They say, Harry sniffs it.

Prince Harry, so they say, is a sniffer.

Cocaine is the drug sniffed by the Prince.

Has he become a drug addict?

Yes.

If he really does sniff.

We cannot verify this information, though.

That's in case somebody decides to sue us.

Next to the article – a slightly out-of-focus iPhone photo of His Royal Highness from some official royal party or suchlike. Here, the editor demonstrates his/her care of those for whom such an information hurricane could be too much to handle. The picture has a caption, sometimes descending to the level of idiotic clarity appropriate for Dora the Explorer or even Peppa Pig, and this too follows a certain format. First, the reader is explained who the main character is, then, after a colon, the gist of the reading. In this case, it'd be *Harry: cocaine sniffing.*

Thus, even the most dyslexic reader is empowered to absorb important news via the simplest of means.

Dear pedagogues and educators, notice that the material is served in a manner that definitely allows much easier understanding and cerebral digestion, thus facilitating mastery of the material. Not only is understanding made easier through repetition (the mother of all knowledge, as they said in ancient Greece) – upon closer inspection, it also turns out that we are dealing with a multi-level educational system here. A beginner might be thrilled to find out that cocaine is a drug, whilst more advanced students can rehearse themselves in different word forms, as in sniff, sniffs, has sniffed, sniffer, sniffing.

And now some concept-checking questions: what the heck is Harry doing? Is he sniffing what? Is he the only one? Admittedly, the last question is somewhat rhetorical and outside the scope of the above publication.

Lithuanians didn't waste their time on crap like this. On the first day, one of them paged through the *Adult Sport* and after observing 'It's got the sport in the title, but mostly sluts inside' threw it away. For the most part, they sat around their own table during the break and chatted in Lithuanian. Vlad-Smigjavicus fled from them like the devil runs from holy water; in the beginning, he even tried to consume his tea break sandwich where he worked, but the foreman forbade this and pointed out that the smell and the crumbs might attract rats. He was deported to the canteen. I tried to cheer him up, even retelling the story of the great times we had had with Rahima in Ireland to remind him of his main motivation, but nothing worked. Rahima had found a job on the 118 118 phone service and slept most of the day as she had a lot of night shifts. Her days off were unpredictable and different every week, so it was difficult to match her schedule with the life rhythm of a builder.

In fact, things were getting gradually worse as regards to Vlad's romance.

The hardest blow of all was the culture shock he suffered. He could handle neither the smell of marijuana coming from Rahima's room nor her returning home late at night completely plastered after a football game watched in a pub. Once she fell over the shoes left in the hall and threw up all over them. Her bisexuality and her open adoration of porn actress Jenna Jamesson made his cheeks change from pink to intense red.

A few times she had friends over, and these English roses completely shattered Vlad's ego. Never before he had stood so close to a British babe – one of those sexy blonde bombshells you see on Friday nights in super-miniskirts and open cleavage, clubbing in places where a cocktail costs more than a labourer's daily wage, then rounding it all off by waking up in a cab with misted windows at four o'clock in the morning and with her mobile phone lost forever. That was Rahima's world, and most of her girlfriends looked as though they had stepped out of the front page of a fashion magazine. Our house and its inhabitants were a different world for them: they inspected us with curiosity, but were too cautious to risk closer contact. To them, Latvia, Lithuania or Ukraine was just a different word for Russia, and it seemed that, by default, they attributed all the traits of the average Russian to anybody from Eastern Europe, assuming them all to be vodka drinkers who shared their towns with bears.

One Friday evening, instead of going to work, Rahima gathered a bunch of blondes and two Spaniards at her place to have a drink before hitting the bars. The Spanish chaps held hands when walking around. The guests spent some three minutes in the living room with the rest of us, while Rahima busied herself in the bathroom right before taking off. To make space so that everyone could have a seat, one of the Spaniards sat on other's lap and was rewarded with a kiss on the chin. Both giggled. We tried to keep up a polite conversation and found out that Rahima had her birthday that day. Loha and Vlad received the news with pained gasps. They felt cruelly ignored, not least because it was clear they weren't invited along because they lacked the language skills and social status to be able to participate anyway. It had, evidently, been automatically agreed that the possibility of them hanging out at an expensive night club with the aboriginal population of the British Isles was quite out of the question. After paying the entrance fee and buying a few drinks they wouldn't have a penny left to send home or meet their share of the rent. And even if they were to go to a club, their chances of charming a female with their conversation were close to zero because of their miserable lack of linguistic skills. They clearly felt they were being mistreated, but Vlad at least found a way to let off steam after Rahima had come down and the chortling and cackling company had buggered off. He turned towards Loha.

"Loha," he muttered in a voice darkened by emotional hurt, "you know what I just saw? I just saw a POOF!"

It appeared that the presence of gays within the circle of friends surrounding the woman of his dreams completely destroyed Vlad's vision of a harmonious family life with her. Utterly shocked, he dashed to the fridge and grabbed a whole four-pack. He needed some moral support, a relief from the pangs of heart and soul he had just experienced.

"In Vinnytsa, they would get their shit kicked out of them in no time," he exclaimed. "A poof is – heck, he is a – whatchucallitagain – a gay! That's what he is! And a gay is a POOF! She has poofy friends!"

See how life works sometimes? Here you are, honest of all builders, sitting around at home at the end of a hard day's night, sipping your well-earned beer, when the young goddess from upstairs smashes all your romantic notions about her. In a few minutes, Vlad's world had been reduced to ruins, all his hopes and dreams stomped on by the campy boots of two Spanish gays. Now as never before he perceived the depth of the cultural differences between them – it was an abyss he could not cross. POOFS were something he could never forgive, that was clear. And it was also clear that money wasn't the only reason he couldn't afford a night out in Soho. There were other reasons, complicated and intangible reasons that would be difficult for him to express verbally; there were things that were perfectly acceptable from a British point of view and totally impossible even to think of from an Eastern European viewpoint. It wasn't just the contrasting attitudes to sex, but everything else as well – the music, the haircuts, the fashion trends... all were absolutely incompatible. Even though some of us have lived in London for years now, we still find ourselves behind an invisible line that separates us in our crowded, shared accommodation with its second-hand furniture from the other London, the city of rich cultural life, stock exchange wealth and Madonna's private mansion.

Some things are just like that. Nothing can be done about it. You can stick your roosterhood into the doorframe and slam the door, yet it won't change a thing. We Eastern Europeans (apart from a random Russian oligarch now and then, of course) can only sweep the street, for a minimum wage. After the colourful pageants and carnivals have passed, all we can do is clean up after them and then sit ourselves down on the pavement kerb to relax with a can of a cheap, frothing bevvy.

After Rahima's birthday, Vlad was depressed for about a week. Then he and Loha decided to move to Bristol, where a friend of Loha's had invited both of them to work in a new Russian restaurant. They needed security personnel there as well as a kitchen porter who would be able to communicate with the chefs in Russian. That made them both ideal candidates. After the trauma over the gay couple, Rahima had lost her value tremendously in Vlad's eyes, and he didn't even talk to her anymore.

Not that they talked much before anyway, but I suppose he felt the change in himself so profoundly he refused even an inner dialogue with her.

The Russian restaurant in Bristol sounded like much more of a plan all of a sudden, and the two of them announced their departure in two weeks' time. The next thing we knew, Lillian moved in with her head chef. She didn't throw any kind of a leaving party. She just waved at us, left her keys and her last contribution to the electricity on the table and closed the door behind her on the way out. She wasn't a huge fan of ours, and we weren't great fans of hers either.

All of a sudden Rahima and I were going to be left alone to pay all the bills. The damn rent contract was enough to suffocate us all by itself. Even though it was still in Grisha Krasko's name, our landlord knew us too well and would demand the rent anyway. We could have left as well, but I personally was working overtime every day and didn't have either the time or the desire to look for another place. Rahima also found the place cheap and reliable, and couldn't be arsed to look for somewhere else. I mentioned to the Lithuanian chippies at work that there were some rooms available at a reasonable price, and lo and behold – not only were they interested, but they were also available two weeks from then, when both the Ukrainians were heading to Bristol. And they even had a car to make the move easier! For every bunch of nasty surprises at least one nice thing comes along. The two weeks rushed and then the ethnic contents of our house were changed once again. The Ukrainians left and the Lithuanians moved in.

In fact, you could say our flat share got richer by five, with four Lithuanians and Jesus, because all four builders (quite remarkably, all carpenters!) belonged to some fashionable new Christian evangelical church. Immediately after getting the first payments down, they made it clear that they expected the kitchen table to be kept clean, that there would be no working on Sundays, that there would be no foul language, and it would be good if everyone would remember to recite a short prayer before meals. Rimantas noticed a guitar in my room and lent me a DVD with a Christian documentary about the satanic influences of rock 'n' roll. Valdas told me one more time about the hidden messages in 'Stairway to Heaven' and changed the Led Zeppelin poster on the bathroom door to a crusade poster featuring Dr Luis Palau. The other two blokes – tall Stan and short Stan – only smiled and nodded in agreement while I was educated in matters concerning the inevitability of the end of the world.

A couple of days later, Rahima turned out to be a cause for concern once again, but in a different way this time. I hadn't paid much attention to it before, but the Lithuanians sniffed it out in an instant – she was a Muslim! Well, not a very pious one, I would have said, as she drank alcohol once in a while and obviously wasn't married to Antonio or any of her other male lovers, never mind the female ones. But the very fact that she would not accept the divine nature of Christ and didn't believe he rose from the dead, woke up the crusaders in our new neighbours. In Islamic tradition, Jesus is regarded merely as a prophet, not the son of God, and it is believed that there will be no more prophets after Mohammad. One of the first things that Jesus will do on Doomsday, according to traditionalist Muslims, will be to clarify his status and correct the misunderstandings invented by Christianity – such as the Resurrection and him being the son of God.

All the Lithuanians spoke English, more or less, and were quite ready to save her from the flames of hell at any time, but she was pretty successful in her devilish tricks to avoid salvation at their hands, made easier by the fact that she mostly worked night shifts. So they took a deep breath and decided to save me first since I was closer at hand.

Chapter 11

Don't start jumping to conclusions. I don't want to lose readers just because some of you guys really keep the religion thing close to your hearts. It's not like I'm denying something or rejecting it. The simple fact of life is that there are gazillions of people out there who are not Christians – so does that mean God has created gazillions of souls knowing very well he is going to send them to roast in hell? Typically, such folks are equally convinced that it's the *Christians* who will get punished after this worldly game is over. Religion is like a lottery: you bet on a particular faith, but you don't know whether your ticket is going to be the right one. After a few weeks in the company of four Lithuanian Christian carpenters their idea of things crystallised in my brain roughly like this: there's St Peter standing by the gate of heaven (or Buddha, or Mohammad, etc. tick own version) with a laptop containing all your life in files – good deeds, bad deeds, sins, prayers, all neatly sorted and saved under respective directories. A poor soul turns up and accounts for its life. Peter (or whoever else that might be in your belief system) ticks all the boxes, as the soul in question has tried from the bottom of its heart to do good, all good and nothing but good. Aha, thinks the soul, what a winner I am, and how great it is going to be, the ultimate bliss of heaven. And then the gatekeeper opens his last, secret software programme that has a login and password unknown to mortals and angels alike, even though they have been gossiping about it for millennia, and fires off questions the soul has no way of predicting.

'Did thou work Sundays? Art thou circumcised? Did thou eat pork? How doth thou make the sign of the cross – with three or four fingers? How many times a year shall we celebrate the festival of the Goddess Kali? What is the optimum number for a human sacrifice to Huitzilopochtli at the annual harvest festival?

Which direction shalt thou face when worshipping the corn god? Who receives the offerings in milk, and who in beer: Zeus, Odin, Thor, Brigantia?'

And let all the deities at once have mercy on you if you screw up just one single time, for behold – humans have been slaying each other in the name of the right answer since the dawn of time! You'll have noticed that most people belong to a certain religion only because they were born in a particular place. Are you personally going to roast in hell because you were born in Baghdad, Iraq, or Lickham Bottom, Devon, England, or Superior Bottom, West Virginia, USA? Either could turn out to be a place where the one true religion has simply never been heard of.

I would like to set down my foot and declare my position: nobody knows, whatever they say. I bet the one who believes in Jah Rastafari does it for real. So does the one who believes that Ra is the one and the scarab is his messenger. So let's stay friendly and hope that if there is something at all on the other side, then at least we'll be reunited with our friends and families. It's pointless to take responsibility for anyone else. Sort yourself out first. You never know – mathematically, there's always a possibility that you have the unlucky ticket in the religious lottery and the person you are trying to convert is actually the lucky ticket holder. Or, simply closer to God than you are.

My new neighbours were alien to such democratic concepts. They took their mission seriously. Obviously, God Himself had made them move into our house as a part of His plan to rescue two souls on the edge of the Lake of Fire.

During one of the first evenings at our place, Rimantas revealed a secret to me that was supposed to change the entire run of my life. The truth, he said, was that I am a sinner and only God could save me from hell. That wasn't much of a news item, but he added an important twist to it: the end of the world was literally around the corner. In fact, I barely had enough time to sort myself out before all hell broke loose.

"It'll be INCREDIBLY bad," he assured me. "It won't be any old end of the world, Hollywood style. No, this time, it will be for real." Rimantas spoke with great certainty as he perched on our kitchen table in a sleeveless shirt and whisked instant coffee powder into a cream. "The sun will die and Satan will grind his teeth. The Revelation of John explains everything, black on white and, by the way, it also describes the signs that will herald the Second Coming of Christ. Most of these signs are fulfilled already."

He finished whisking his coffee into a thick cream and put the kettle on. (In case you're interested: two teaspoons of instant coffee, two of sugar, and one and a half of water, then whisk it energetically till it looks almost like custard, then – whoooosh – fill the cup with boiling water so that you end up with delicious black water with a frothy head. Or you could just eat the cream without adding the water).

Outside, the birds sang, as per typical English afternoon. I knew Rahima would soon be getting up to take her shower before leaving for work, so it was a good idea to go for a leak before it was too late. I was still drinking beer after work even though the cold stares of the Lithuanians were telling me without words that alcoholism is a sin. Whatever. I had been living there long before them, and I had my human rights to defend. Besides, because of them I had quit smoking inside the house and now was doing it in the garden. I mumbled some words of excuse and got my ass up to go and make my bladder gladder, as they say.

"Aha!" Said Rimantas. "You too, Willis."

That's what they called me – Willis. I didn't think it was the correct version of William in Lithuanian, but I let it be.

"What?" I asked.

"Nothing special. You see, most people on this planet are possessed by demons. Like now – you think you want to go for a leak, yet these are actually demons whispering in your ear, saying you want to piss. The reason for that is really simple – demons know their time on earth is almost finished. They hear what we are talking about now and they know that I am able to save you. That's why they try to distract you."

"Rahima is going to get up soon and take a shower. She always does at this time. And I've had a couple of beers, you know."

"Let's leave that woman out of it, hey? She belongs to the vanguard of Satan's army. By the way, in your case demons are making use of the standard kit of weaknesses – bodily urges, women, alcohol…"

I sat down wearily. The kettle clicked, accompanied by the sound of boiling water. Rimantas poured the water into his cup. With a hiss, the cream rose atop the black liquid.

"OK, say what you have to say. I'll go for a leak later."

"Hallelujah! You just made a small but significant victory. Congratulations!"

He clinked his coffee mug against my beer can.

"The truth is simple yet complicated, scary yet beautiful, all at the same time. The Lord Himself has said that when the Day of Judgement comes near, He will give signs to alert the true believers. And here they are." Rimantas made a wide circle with one hand, apparently encompassing the whole world. "Why has science developed so much during the last couple of centuries? Just think of it, all these discoveries and innovations in rapid succession. Whachya think? It's because the Archfiend has understood he hasn't got much time left to rule this world. That's why he has invented nanotechnology. The secret government of the world is gonna implant microchips under the skin of the right hand of every single person and keep information on everybody in their files – name, surname, National Insurance number, bank account, etcetera. You simply walk into a supermarket, scan your hand – and the balance is paid. No need for cash or even a bank card, so they say. But for the Beast, that's just another way of collecting souls, because the implants will allow Satan to influence people's mood and thoughts. They are coding people to choose who will take Satan's side during the last battle of Armageddon. For the end is nigh. Do you know how we can tell that all of this is true?"

I didn't. Instead, I knew something else – that I wasn't going to get relief any time soon, because I just heard a door slamming upstairs; Rahima had gone to take her shower. The only thing that was left now was to relax and find the most comfortable position on the chair to lessen the pressure.

Rimantas took a jar of instant coffee from the table and turned the rear side of it towards me.

"See the bar code? All the bars have numbers at the bottom. Under the first, the last and the middle bars there are no numbers, right? In the Satanic system of computation, the secret numbers for those bars are: six, six and six. The supermarket shopping system was created by the Evil One, and each time you buy something, that confirms his power. Never has the fight for human souls been as bitter as it is now, and it happens in Tesco and Sainsbury's more than anywhere else, my friend. For Satan is trying to pull as many souls together with him into the Lake of Fire as he can. That's what the rise of technology is about."

"Are you saying all scientists are either stupid or Satanists?"

Rimantas pulled a face. "Scientists, whee! They are just showing off with their telescopes, microscopes, sonars and what not, yet they don't know the simplest things. Just use your head – think! For instance, everybody knows there is gravity. So, if there is gravity and earth has a pulling force, the moon would have crashed into the earth a long time ago! Scientists know that, yet they keep their mouths shut. Why is the moon still up in the sky?" Rimantas paused dramatically and gave me a taunting look.

I tried to recall what we had been taught in secondary school about planetary movement, but I had to admit I wasn't prepared with an answer.

Rimantas smiled and explained it to me like he was speaking to a little child. "Because God is holding it there! Only God is able to hold something so big so high."

There was a silence for a while. I simply didn't know what to say.

"If you think with your own head for a while, everything falls into place. No scientists, presidents or prime ministers will be able to lead you astray anymore." Rimantas leant forward, his eyes glowing and his breath smelling of instant Nescafé. "Willis, I like you quite a lot. I think you're a good chap deep inside and deserve to live longer than a few weeks. I will reveal a secret to you, and do us a favour – tell it to everybody you ever meet. Remember, there was a lot of noise and hysteria when the year 2000 was coming up? What was it? I'll tell you what it was. A Satanic provocation! Just think for a moment – there never was a year zero in the calendar, right? The implications are clear. Two-thousand years since the birth of Christ will be not in the year 2000, but in the year 2001! And that is now, my friend. Satan wanted everybody to go bonkers in the year 2000, when nothing was bound to happen, so they would relax and sit back when the real Armageddon happened. See? Ask, and you will be answered! Pray, and you will be saved!"

The air in our little kitchen had become thick and energised. The end was obviously damn nigh. Angels were polishing their trumpets and combing the feathers on their wings; demons were sharpening their fangs on massive grinding stones, and the Prince of Darkness was using his laptop to programme scientists to destroy the world. I shook my head. The prospects were truly grim.

And then, completely unexpectedly, Nansen turned up on our doorstep. While in the forest, he had developed a business plan.

Chapter 12

All in all, Nansen had been doing pretty well. Nature is beautiful, he told us. Also, he had found out that at a school next to his forest hideout the European Union were running a free English evening course, and he was determined to graduate. This would be the first step towards him leaving the construction game and maybe even becoming an English teacher one day.

But there had been a downside, too, and sometimes he had had to pay a hefty price to learn a lesson or two about eco-tramping. Crucially, he had lost the option of living a whole month on a sack of rice or potatoes, as many Eastern Europeans do. So, initially at least, all the money he had saved on rent had been spent on ready meals he bought at the local supermarket to heat up in the microwave in the *stroika* canteen, plus different snacks to eat while in the bush, for there was no gas or electricity in his camp. As a result, the fifteen-hundred pounds he owed to different people had proved difficult to save. So, out of his next weekly salary of two-hundred and fifty pounds he had bought himself a pair of leather trousers for a hundred and eighty. His reasoning was that you don't have to wash them as often as jeans, allowing him to save the time he normally spent travelling to friends with washing machines – which in the long run would increase his ability to pay off his debts.

To compensate for the money he had spent on trousers, Nansen worked out a scheme for saving on food. Around that time, Lidl were filling their shelves with two-litre tins of marinated tomatoes. Nansen had bought two, eaten all the contents, and torn the paper labels off. This gave him two saucepans – one for food, the other for coffee, which was something he had been addicted to from his teens. Starbucks's is quite expensive, you know, with one cup costing nearly the same as a whole pack of roasted coffee in Lidl. This had been another hard blow to his wallet.

Unfortunately, the saucepan scheme had also ended in fiasco. There were absolutely no wires available in the forest, or even at work, that could be used to make a handle. So he had had to place the tomato cans directly on the burning firewood. Even though it worked sometimes, more often than was desirable the pan would turn turtle and spill half-ready soups and stews into the flames. I shall also add, sensitively, that Nansen had to finish four litres of marinated tomatoes within a day, otherwise they would rot in the humid environment of the park, so rich in microbial forms of life. The result was that he soon ran out of paper supplies in his camp and his work performance was severely hampered for a few days. He also had to skip some English lessons, too, as the loud rumbling of his inner self would noticeably destroy the atmosphere in class.

The last blow came when he decided to switch from the tin saucepans to wooden skewers. In the form of twigs, these were growing everywhere in the park. Using these, he lived mostly on mushrooms and meat reduced to clear from the supermarket. Yet the open fire had added to his builder's odour a hint of peaty forest soil and the pungency of the solid British oak he used to burn. This wasn't a particular problem at work, as a lot of people stink on building sites, especially the labourers. It's all part of our job. The proletarian aristocracy like the carpenters, plumbers, plasterers and especially the managerial folks sometimes smell better, like orchids, because they can afford to buy themselves deodorants with truly murderous force. But it was a different matter at school. To explain his smoky odour, Nansen had told his classmates that he worked as a gardener and often had to burn old leaves.

This story was not accepted, however, by the little green men, otherwise known as the wardens. One day they entered Nansen's camping site and insisted on him leaving immediately. And so Nansen did, and what is more, the new place he found was even better. It had a swampy spot nearby with something like a well in the middle of it. On dry days, Nansen was able to access the well without getting his feet wet and draw a refreshing sip from the very bowels of Mother Earth as all around him the nettles and grasses shook and undulated with the winds.

But working on the site was tiring and living in a nylon tent in the forest was less healthy than it sounds. As a result of all these inconveniences, he had come to the obvious conclusion that a change needed to be made. As procrastination is the thief of time he had come straight to us and, after a shower, proposed that we smuggle cigarettes.

To be fair, everybody was smuggling or at least selling ciggies those days, although some operated on a bigger scale than others. Back in the good old times, a pack of twenty Marlboro in Eastern Europe would have cost from forty pence upwards, a price never as brutal as in Britain, where smokers had to part from a whole five pounds for a pack of twenty. We always grabbed as many blocks of two-hundred as we could on our visits home, thus often covering our ticket money and maybe even earning a little on top. The low-level smugglers would bring in two blocks of two-hundred each and sell them in packs of twenty at a time among their friends and work colleagues. Usually, it was cheap stuff like LM or Lucky Strike. More serious guys transported up to several tens of thousands of blocks a month and sold them to corner shops. Nansen was aiming at the middle level for starters: he would be my courier, doing the practical part of actually getting the cigarettes into the UK and bringing them back to sell to some corner shop owners he had heard might be interested. My role was more honorary and financial, meaning I had to buy him plane tickets and give him money for some hundred blocks of two-hundred Marlboro since that's a pretty trendy brand, well-known and loved by most smokers regardless of ethnicity and nationality. If the plan went wrong, I had nothing to lose, Nansen insisted, as it would be him who would face the hardship of punishment should things go pear-shaped. I just had to invest and then receive fifty per cent of the income.

Theoretically, the plan wasn't bad, but I had just returned from Latvia myself and had hardly any money left. It was obvious that Nansen didn't want to wait. He graciously combed his long black hairdo with all ten fingers, and an innocent smile lit up his Jesus-like bearded face.

"All right," he said as he changed position in his chair, leather trousers squeaking expressively. He threw one leg over the other, briefly drawing my attention to dusty sandals on his feet. 'Then let's sell some cannamilk.'

Everybody knows about cannabis sativa/indica and its traditional use – the smoking of the dried parts of the unfertilised female plant. It is also a well-known fact that the usual European cannabis plant, aka hemp, the kind that grows on the edge of your gutter, produces no enjoyable sensations when smoked, even if it is be the biggest and most beautiful female with the largest buds in your backyard. Enter the Soviet school of life. In Soviet times, psychedelic enthusiasts in Latvia went through various challenges to overcome the problem of supply and finally achieved significant results through various alternatives. As an alternative to marijuana, young folks on the eastern side of the Iron Curtain smoked banana skins; as an alternative to magic mushrooms they ate fly agaric; as an alternative to heroin, they injected hanka – poppy buds and stems boiled in a distilled paint solvent; and as an alternative to hashish yoghurt, European hemp was boiled in milk till it turned green. I've also heard that there are real magic mushrooms in the national parks around Moscow, but that's a bit risky. If you're a non-specialist, the chances are you'll contract either diarrhoea or paralysis of your breathing apparatus. Or worse still, die from both simultaneously.

In Soviet times, when information from the West was scarce, there were very few hippies in all of the USSR, as there was practically no informational basis for that kind of subculture – even listening to the Western radio was illegal. Instead, drugs were consumed mostly in prisons and among professional criminals. For instance, the *chefyr* was relatively popular, since all the ingredients were available even in a prison. You filled a cup full of loose tea and poured boiling water in to the brim. Then you covered it with a plate and gently heated for ten minutes, before drinking all the liquid and eating the tea leaves with a spoon. It worked a bit like ecstasy and kept you agitated and an insomniac for a couple of days. Since some hippies actually ended up being in prison for living a non-Soviet lifestyle (for example, being unemployed was a criminal offence, a truly effective measure in tackling unemployment), it was behind the bars where prison and hippy subcultures met and mixed, creating somewhat interesting hybrids at times. Our generation luckily didn't need to go to prison to scratch the theory together – it was enough to hang out with the chosen few who actually had managed to acquire vinyl with The Doors or Jefferson Airplane during the Soviet times, and then had done a time for it. If Jim Morrison had planted the longing in the hearts of our older hippies, Soviet penal system and prison experience had provided them with the means to satisfy that longing, and as fledging rockers ourselves, we had listened and learnt. Nansen reckoned we should put it to the test.

"Across the field next to my new camping site there is a dried-up gutter," he told me. "If you jump over, there is a little house in ruins and nothing else, except lots of wild hemp everywhere. There are some occasional nettles there as well, but never mind. We could boil tens of litres of cannamilk and make some decent dough."

Well, money for milk – that much we certainly should be able to raise. But where would we sell the end product? Normally weed is sold in Camden Town, where Bob Marley, weird handbags and 'Free Tibet!' stickers are rather the norm. Of course, we could stand there with a bucket and simply scoop out plastic cups of the stuff for five pounds apiece, but the smell and colour would be sort of a giveaway to the police. Nansen's answer was simple – we'd check out squat parties and illegal raves, the ones that happen secretly in places where people disinterested in drugs simply never appear. Plus, there might be some interesting bands and DJs performing.

Admittedly, the idea had potential. With cannamilk, you can boil plant of any sex and at any stage and any season, as long as it is hemp. Sure, we would have to boil it at my place, otherwise we risked Nansen's saucepans toppling over in the flames and the entire brew being wasted. We decided to do it next Sunday, while my flatmates were in church. Meanwhile, we had to find the nearest squat and find out whether they were about to have a celebration any time soon and if they could be potentially interested in some cannamilk.

Since Nansen still dwelled in his lonesome tent on the edge of the forest, it was also up to me to find the squat. Unexpectedly, Rahima offered help. When I mentioned to her that I was looking for a squat somewhere nearby, she had an immediate suggestion. There was a place in Hackney, she said, where they organised events for open-minded people. When I enquired cautiously about drugs, she shook her beautiful pitch-black hair and smiled. Absolutely, she said – you could get whatever you wanted in that place, and you could also sell some as long as you acted respectfully towards the people who were already in the business. It was a place of free love and mutual respect.

"I've met some brilliant people there,'" she said and gave me another enigmatic and erotic smile, as only Asian women can.

I had no doubt about Rahima's ability to meet the most random people in most random places. Sometimes she brought them over to our house. Despite the rhythm of her life being so different from mine, I had met some of the fellows with whom she once in a while shared short, yet very passionate, moments. Anybody who has experienced an aroused couple behind their bedroom wall will certainly understand what I mean. Squeaky bed springs, the rhythmic thud of the head banging against the wall or the headboard, isn't the worst – probably what gets on your nerves most is the continuous moaning and especially the recital of 'Oh my God, oh my God'. If they are in a mood for lengthy foreplay or if the lad is capable of an enduring performance, the OMG part ceases for a bit – just long enough for you to drift back to sleep or to reading your book – and then picks up again with renewed energy. Absolutely crazy. I had noticed that Clemente, a tall and friendly chap from Nicaragua, with whom Rahima had sex more often than with anybody else, caused her to moan with a rather low intensity but for longer periods of time. I suppose I should have respected him for that. Thank God, he could make her moan so quietly you could simply turn the music up a bit louder and be OK. Then there were some Asian guys who apparently weren't able to do so well, at least judging by the noise made, so I saw them only a couple of times. At the top of the scale, I guess, was Mo – a tall, muscular Nigerian who usually visited on Sunday afternoons when Clemente was at work selling sandwiches. Rahima would squeal with excitement when he arrived at the front door. Then the door to her room was slammed and within some thirty seconds the rhythmic OMG would begin. It would reach a crescendo in some two minutes and then stop; the guy obviously had a talent in being an express service, calling all stations to orgasm in next to no time, or going straight to orgasm only. Usually, when I heard the doorbell and Mo's voice, I went for a fag in the garden. Since I prefer roll-ups, that usually filled the time while they got on with their socialising. By the time I had rolled my ciggie, puffed on out slowly for a bit and then returned to the kitchen to put the kettle on, they were done. Once I even met Mo in the living room on his way out.

Rahima herself called her boys 'guy friends', to distinguish them from the girls she would go to bed with. I suppose 'boyfriend' sounded too limiting and official to her. The most intelligent and the nicest by far was Clemente. He wore round, Lennon-style glasses and had longish black hair tied in a ponytail. He was really friendly and talkative and socialised with everybody, including the Lithuanians, nodding in an understanding manner when they preached at him. He said he was studying to become an IT specialist and was intending to go into the internet business after graduation.

Luckily enough, most of Rahima's friends came around on Saturdays or Sundays, the days the Lithuanians devoted to the Lord. Even though it was none of my business, I instinctively felt they would not approve of her variety of sexual partners. On top of that, Rahima quite enjoyed having a drink or a spliff right before the action started. The Nicaraguan always brought gin and tonic with him when visiting. Once Rahima mentioned that whatever was left after Clemente had gone, she used to give to her other lovers. I asked her once how many men she had been with since arriving in London. She scratched the tattooed dragon on her shoulder thoughtfully.

"Seven. Eight, actually. There is a chap from my work, but he fucking wants to marry me. Pisses me off."

Clemente also wanted to marry her. What a nuisance.

So that was the routine of my life. Work and religious talk during the week, with a busty nymphomaniac rhythmically moaning on the other side of the wall for added variety at weekends. I felt stuck. The UK was supposed to be a country that offered opportunities to those who were smart enough to grab them – there had to be something else I could do apart from eating dust on construction jobs.

So to the squat party I went, to find out whether anybody would be interested in buying some cannamilk.

Chapter 13

As much as London is predictably dangerous and unfriendly towards cyclists, it is surprisingly welcoming to squatters. Back then, squatting was pretty well organised and, one might say, almost completely legally supported. The famous Jamaican squats in central London are a good example. If you're interested, see the friendly squatters' advice team in Whitechapel: the London Squatters' Union is always happy to help. In some places, people have been squatting for years, paying bills, organising community events, running evening classes, growing strawberries and carrots on roof terraces and pot in illuminated basements. If they are not paying rent, often the karmic logic dictates they should at least clean up the area, sell cheap vegetarian food or teach kids drawing lessons. It is a way of life where personal freedom and artistic expression are very important. Squat parties sometimes have the best DJs, as well as the most peculiar bands and amazing vegan food. Although squatters usually tend to be politically active and are regularly involved in demonstrations, strikes and so on, they are otherwise generally very peaceful and friendly. It may be a bit of an idealistic picture, but that was the everyday reality in most Western European squats at least.

I was glad that the squat Rahima invited me to what was a *classique* version, one with psychedelic images on the walls and Free Tibet! Posters on the doors. The three-storey house stood behind a massive brick wall and had a couple of dead trees by the front door adorned with fairy lights and Aum signs. It was quite obviously a good place to settle down, as it was next to a park and away from other residential houses, thus allowing the opportunity to be a bit noisier than was usually acceptable. It was quite discreet, too; the brickwork bore only a couple of examples of Aum graffiti, and the real independent art was revealed only once you had passed the gate. Even the rainbow flag was hung above the entrance door at a low angle so not to attract the eye of lazy onlookers.

Inside, almost any item within reach had been painted or decorated one way or another, including even the scissors the kinky girl with green hair and rows of rings in each eyebrow used to snip off self-made tickets for us. The spacious rooms provided ample room for two DJs and their decks and a bar with cheap lager and vegetarian snacks. Musically, the choice was between dub and trance. I liked the dub room better since it had more decoration and real paintings on the walls, including some realistic cannabis vignettes on columns and in the corners. There were also omnipresent aliens painted with massive eyes and egg-shaped heads. Not too bad, really, with probably more than a touch of acid or magic mushrooms for inspiration.

Rahima and I took a pint each and sat our asses down on pillows in bright yellow cases under green sheets that stretched from one column to another. The DJ obviously felt bass-inclined; his rhythmic daba-daba-booms shook our ribcages, intertwined with the rattling of a programmed snare drum.

Soon Rahima presented me to the people who ran the place, and we started to chat about weed. "Oh, I have some," said a skinny, middle-aged man with Maori tattoos all over his face and he produced an ivory-adorned wooden box full of high quality marijuana. A wave of smell washed over the room as he opened it. When we took our first puff, others could have got stoned simply by standing next to us and breathing in deeply. I asked casually whether they would mind me bringing in my own material next time. The skinny bloke (his name was Stu) frowned slightly, but the fact that I was Rahima's flatmate obviously helped to establish the rapport, so I was given the benefit of the doubt. That's all right, he said, but I would have to respect the local tradition of peace and friendliness. No aggression. And if I was determined to make money here, it would be only fair if as a newcomer I donated ten per cent of my income towards the squat's maintenance expenses.

I was happy with that. You had to start somewhere. It also seemed that Stu might have all the knowledge and connections we might need. Judging by the attitude of everybody else towards him, Stu was clearly the leader there. I promised that the locals would get some cannamilk for free – according to Nansen, the cannabis fields behind his tent were simply vast – and we changed the subject to ska artists Warsaw Poland Brothers. Rahima was a huge fan.

We returned home around five o'clock in the morning. Rahima brought with her an Argentinian bloke with sexy stubble and curly hair, black as coal, and an accent so strong it sometimes changed into full Spanish. That seemed to have quite an effect on Rahima, as she laughed a lot and kept playing around with this hair. Be that as it may, I had enough beer and marijuana inside me to switch off as soon as my head touched the pillow, so no OMG disturbed me. In any case, I had developed a helpful technique to guarantee a good night's sleep: before going to bed I would leave a pair of shoes within easy reach and if the OMG started up, I would throw one shoe, then the next one if necessary. It saved me getting up and knocking on the wall.

We got down to work the very next weekend. The boiling part is quite a smelly enterprise, so we worked out a scheme that would annoy the Lithuanians as little as possible. Nansen was to get a day off on Friday and arrive early in the morning, soon after we had all gone to work. I would leave the key for him under the flower pot by the front door. His job was to bring the weed over, boil it in the big shiny saucepan we normally kept under the kitchen sink, then ventilate the house by opening all the windows, burn some Indian incense sticks, fill the ready produce in plastic milk bottles, hide them under my bed, and then go for a walk. He would turn up after working hours and then we would go to the squat party, this time with some cannamilk to sell.

On the day in question, I did my best to get home earlier than the Lithuanians. Nansen had fulfilled almost all parts of the plan, but only almost. He had taken a day off, gathered a massive amount of hemp in his tourist rucksack and arrived in Leyton. On the train, he hid in the toilet to dodge the train fare and to hide away the bag, which in the warm atmosphere of the carriage was emanating a strong, characteristic smell. When I arrived, the green brew was already made and hidden under my bed in four-pint milk bottles. Nansen was gone, leaving the house reeking of burned milk, cannabis and something less tangible, but disturbingly reminiscent of burned human hair. Rahima was running around the kitchen like an angry tigress. She had to be at work soon, she yelled at me, and all this shit was getting on her nerves. The stench had woke her up an hour early. All her clothes now stank of burned pig carcass. The reference to a pig carcass was obviously meant to underline for me the level of stress she was suffering, offending her Muslim sensibilities on both emotional and religious grounds. Things had gone badly awry.

I opened all the windows, something Nansen had forgotten to do, and lit up the incense sticks he had left by the stove. Needless to say, he had forgotten about them too. When Rahima finally left, still fuming and cussing, I sprayed some toilet air freshener around the kitchen. Then I thought for a while before going into the garden and lighting up a pile of old rubbish deposited by the garden fence. It contained some old rags and eggshells, which could explain the stench. It all burned pretty well as the last few days had been dry and sunny. As soon as I heard the Lithuanians opening the door, I ran out in the garden with a jug and poured it over the fire. The whole place was full of smoke.

Valdas was first to enter the kitchen and spot me through the open garden door.

"What are you doing?" he asked in surprise.

"Must be the stupid neighbours throwing cigarette butts onto our rubbish," I explained, trying to sound angry. "Half of London stinks now."

"It does," Valdas agreed. "Whatta people. Phee! Let's close the door. Look, all the windows are open, too! I'm gonna explain some household basics to that Islamist woman tomorrow. It stinks outside, and she opens all the windows! Let's close them quickly."

I was trying to figure out how to prevent Valdas from doing this when Tall Stan appeared next to him.

"What's going on?"

"Look, someone has set fire to the rubbish pile in the garden," Valdas said angrily. "That's where that stench is coming from."

"Oh. What are those weeds in the sink then? They also seem to stink a bit."

Bloody Nansen! Everybody's eyes turned to me since I was the first to come home, but at that very moment, I was saved by the master brewer himself knocking on the main door. I went to answer it, thus avoiding any tricky questions for now. As soon as I opened the door, Nansen closed his nostrils with one hand and pulled a face.

"Fuck, are you guys crazy? What's that reek?"

Alas, there is no justice in the world. I wanted to scream, 'It's you, Nansen! YOU did this!' But I had to keep calm in the interests of our conspiracy. One guy creates shit and some other guy has to clean it up afterwards. Usually me. I hastily got him upstairs to prevent him from saying anything else stupid, and then cleaned the milk-soaked cannabis leaves and stems out of the sink. Just in case, I threw it all into the neighbours' bin across the street.

All we had to do now was to toss the bottles in the rucksack and head to the squat before anybody decided to pick up the conversation where we had left off. The problem was, though, that neither of us had had a chance to try the finished product. We needed to know if it worked and was actually drinkable. I had a slight suspicion Nansen might have done something wrong. I didn't remember there being such a stench when we had boiled cannabis in our youth.

"OK, have a sip," said Nansen once we were both in my bedroom. He got a bottle out and we squinted at its contents. The liquid shone through the plastic in alarmingly green tones. There were darker pieces of stem floating around and slowly sinking towards the bottom. Suddenly, I didn't like the idea.

"Better you first. You're screwed up enough already, even when you're sober. You must be, to fill the whole house with that stench and forget the weed in the sink. Besides, my English is better, and I need to be sober to be able to sell the stuff."

Nansen argued for a short while but then took a big gulp.

"How is it?"

"Nothing yet, but you can't expect anything to happen right away, you know. I feel a bit vomity, though."

He was right, nothing happened right away. He nearly threw up only when the bus made a big turn off the Leyton High Road. As always, we were sitting on the upper deck at the front, to enjoy the view. As the driver manoeuvred his machine through the traffic and dodged around the cars it seemed more than once that we were going to hit a lamppost or a pub sign. When the bus took a massive lurch to the left, Nansen suddenly kicked the wall as if pushing the brakes, and grabbed the yellow rail in front of him.

"Will, you moron, look where you're driving!"

I stared at him and he looked back at me, then gave a short, silly giggle as he realised his mistake. We got off the bus before it was too late, and walked the rest of the way. Nansen breathed deeply. He said that helped.

"It must have been that stupid bus," he reassured me. "It was just shaking about too much; nothing to do with the milk. Yet I do feel a bit funny, you know. My arms feel like they're made of rubber."

I bought each of us a kebab, as Nansen said he had the munchies, and we walked on down to the squat. On the way, Nansen started to become a little weird. He was experiencing various indescribable changes in the state of his mind and body, which he tried to put unsuccessfully into words. The effects emerged at least thirty minutes after intake. I decided that this must be a good sign. Never mind the bus – this cannamilk was definitely going to be a seller.

Chapter 14

All began very well. As soon as we mentioned Stu's name to the green-haired maiden at the entrance, she let us in. Through the open door we heard the booming baseline of 'Another one bites the dust' by Queen. It struck me as rather a mainstream choice for the establishment, but once we entered the room everything became clear. A bunch of fellas, in leather costumes, were enjoying themselves jumping up and down to the rhythm. They were all pushing forty and dressed in leather caps, trousers and jackets with lots of zippers that glinted in the psychedelic lighting. No doubt, the guys were enjoying a return to the days of their youth.

The song ended.

'Stayin' alive, stayin' alive' continued the sentimental seventies theme. Stu appeared, his tattooed face all pink and happy and his yellowish teeth bared in an excited smile. He had obviously been high for quite a while already. He waved us over as soon as he noticed us.

"Come here, lads! Meet Emil!"

Emil turned out to be one of the guys in leather jackets. He was quite an athletic geezer and his leather cap had a shiny metal thing on it. The only accessory that was lacking was a whip. He had a blonde hairdo and a German accent and seemed to be in charge of this company of merry men.

"Will has brought an interesting drink with him," Stu shouted in Emil's ear. "First cup for free, innit, Will?"

I was thrilled to find everybody so welcoming and friendly. All because of Rahima, bless her. Well done, Stu! An advertisement cup for free—why not? We went behind the bar and filled up the plastic cups they used to sell spiced Indian teas. The jacketed fellas gathered around the bar, had a shot each, and then returned to the dance floor. I tried a sip myself. It wasn't tasty, if you know what I mean, but other than that it was all right. For a brief moment, there was a strange rubbery feeling in my arms, but the dose was too small to feel anything more than a slight weakness.

Nansen disappeared into the next room and in a while returned with another geezer. What a coincidence, he was Latvian too. His name was Askolds; he wore a suit and a tie and was perfectly shaved. It was the first time I saw an eastern European looking like that. I offered Askolds a cup of cannamilk, but he just shook his head.

"Thanks, I've already had some mushrooms. I'll be all right!"

Mushrooms, right. I looked at Nansen. Maybe that explained the strange, uneasy happiness in his eyes.

"Nansen, you didn't eat any shrooms, did you?" I yelled at him over the voice of Sinead O'Connor.

"Shrooms? You want some? I still have some left."

Nansen ferreted in his inside pocket and produced a plastic box containing the pasty and compressed bodies of mushrooms with orange caps.

Damn squat parties! For fuck's sake!

A couple of the leather jackets came over and asked for some more milk. So far, it works a bit funny—no high, just a weird weakness in the arms, they said. *Arms of rubber*, I thought to myself, and poured some more for the enthusiasts. I was more concerned about the fact that Nansen soon wouldn't be able to distinguish the walls from the ceiling. Actually, that shouldn't be a problem in itself—after all, that's what squat parties are for—yet I felt somewhat responsible for our business plan. I forced myself to relax. There was a nice, free atmosphere to the place. The people around us seemed interested in our milk, and it looked like we were going to make some money out of our European cannabis, handpicked in the wilderness of a park. Everything should be marvellous.

But, alas, Providence had other plans.

Emil turned up with a plastic glass full of beer and used a quieter moment between songs for a brief chat.

"Usually, weed works on me much better with some alcohol," he explained. "Where are you from?"

"Latvia."

"*Ach so, Lettland!*"

"And where are you from?"

"Berlin! The best city in the world, you know."

I cast a quick glance at Nansen. The shrooms were obviously taking over his brain cells. His smile was growing larger and larger, and the pupils of his eyes were growing along with it. I scanned the room. It appeared that the milk had had some impact on the dance style, with everyone moving their arms around a lot as though imitating waves at sea. Cool. At least no one could say it didn't work.

Oh, if only the waving and rubbery feeling had been the only side-effects! At some point, a chubby lad in leather shorts walked up to Emil and shouted something in his ear with a really grim facial expression.

"*Was?*[26]"Emil looked unpleasantly surprised.

"*Ja, ja,*[27]" the lad nodded, pointing at another geezer next to him, who also looked unhappy. Now he pointed at me with an evil look. Out of the darkness of the dance floor emerged a couple more pissed-off faces.

"*Lass uns die Letten erschlagen!*"[28] one of the newcomers yelled.

Before anyone could move, Stu appeared out of nowhere and jumped between us.

"No trouble, please! Calm down, you guys! Is there a problem?"

"Yes, there is!" Emil looked really upset. "My friends are saying they have a diary!"

"Excuse me?" Stu looked as baffled as I was.

"Diary! Watery, absolutely uncontrollable... *Verdammt*[29]!"

Emil spun around on his heel and hastily crossed the dance floor towards the door.

I started to get it, finally.

"I think he means diarrhoea," I mumbled. "They have diarrhoea from the milk because these morons drank beer on top of it."

---

[26] What? (German)

[27] Yes, yes.*(German)*

[28] Let's beat up the Latvians! *(German)*

[29] Damn! (German)

"Exactly, diarrhoea!" the chubby lad in shorts screamed. "Whatta fuck you selling us?"

It felt like offence would be my best defence, so I yelled back at him. "Why did you have to drink beer on top? Only crazies mix milk with lager!"

"But we are crazies!" the chubby lad shouted. "Beer usually helps cannabis take effect!"

"Yeah, but not milk! Milk plus beer adds an assquake super-effect!"

"We demand our money back!"

"You haven't paid anything yet!"

Before Stu could intervene, the chubby lad launched himself at me with an obviously murderous intent. The many zippers of his sleeve scythed the air close to my ear as he collapsed in a heap in front of me.

"My hands feel like robber! I can't hold anything," he cried.

Enough's enough. Even his clumsy English wasn't entertaining anymore. I grabbed the rucksack, threw the milk bottles in, and headed towards the door.

"Don't forget your friend," Stu shouted after me.

I turned around. Nansen was standing apart from everybody, leaning against a column and moving his chin up and down to the rhythm of The Residents. He seemed utterly oblivious of the conflict that threatened to break out. Askolds was sitting on the floor in front of him, contemplating the patterns in the carpet. I walked up to them. Their timing could hardly have been worse, what with the mushrooms reaching maximum effect just as we were being forced to leave.

"Guys, we must bugger off. Emil is angry with us."

No reaction.

I shouted louder: "Nansen, we've got to leave!"

He gave me a charming smile in reply and hugged me round my shoulders. I tried to get him over towards the exit, but it seemed that not only his arms were made of rubber, but his whole body too. Emil reappeared at the far end of the room, slamming the toilet door behind him. The metal thingy on his leather cap glinted in the disco lights like the flashing lights of a cop car. I gripped Nansen around the waist and somehow got him out into the yard.

"Nansen, wake up, NANSEN!"

"Eeeeh."

Nansen's smile grew more and more cute and childish, to the point where it started to become slightly scary. Then he experienced an explosion of uncontrollable laughter. He slipped out of my arms, sat down on the pavement, and laughed, laughed and laughed. Stu came out of the door, steering Askolds in my direction.

"You must disappear," he advised us. The Maori tattoos on his face seemed to be darker than before, or maybe he just was pale with anger. "I hate to have aggression in my squat."

"Uuuuuh, hi hihihi," Nansen giggled from the pavement. His mind had obviously reached the stage where the psychedelic takes over completely. The cannamilk must be enriching the mushroom experience. At least he hadn't had a beer, thank God, like those German twats.

I managed to get all three of us out of sight on the other side of the brick wall. Neither Nansen nor Askolds were in any condition to go further. Marvellous. Instead of making big bucks selling drugs, I had to spend my own money on a cab, into which I loaded both shroomers.

Approaching the same traffic lights that had almost made him puke earlier, Nansen suddenly became strangely clear-minded. Strangely, because only partially.

"Will, are we in a taxi?"

"Yeah, in a cab."

"Askolds, we're in a taxi! Hey, listen, Will, we got to get off. We're going to a pub."

The cab stopped at the red light.

"Will, let's go to a pub! Hey, Askolds, Will is inviting us for a pint, didja hear?"

Askolds only smiled idiotically and loosened his tie a bit. Before I could react, Nansen had the cab door open and had jumped out in the road. Luckily there weren't too many cars around.

"You idiot, where are you going?" I shouted in despair.

Askolds, meanwhile, had followed the crowd instinct and was also out of the car.

"Take it easy, mate," he advised me. "It's fate that we had to leave. But now we've received an order to go to the pub. C'mon."

"The pubs are about to close—it's late. Get back in the cab!"

"Will, we can't. We have instructions, see."

"What fucking instructions?"

Askolds raised a finger solemnly. "There are higher powers than you or me. Fungus, the Mushroom God."

I glanced at the traffic lights, then back at the cars behind us. The amber was about to turn green. Screw it.

"Go wherever you want," I snarled and slammed the door, trying to ignore the slightly rubbery feeling in my arms.

Even though I hadn't planned to take a cab that day, it was actually a great relief to get home in comfort. When we pulled up at the house, I saw that it had been decorated with flower chains and there was a bunch of people outside holding candles. I paid the driver and got out of the car.

"Aaaah, Willis, it's you."

As tall and self-important as ever, Rimantas towered over those standing at the front door. "We are here on a remarkably sad occasion. A good friend of ours, a saint of a man and a good Christian, has passed away. Come with us and have a drop of grape juice. I'm sure you'll be happy to help us remember our mate tonight."

Oh, right, sectarians don't drink alcohol. After promising politely to come down in a short while after going upstairs to get rid of my bag, I climbed up the stairs and stumbled into my bedroom without turning the light on. All I really wanted was darkness and peace. I felt tired and a failure.

I opened the window, leant against the sill and took in a deep gulp of London's humid air. Outside, our apple tree moved gently in the wind. Was it my fault that some people were stupid enough to mix beer and milk? Some people think all you need to do is just wolf down whatever makes you high, and that's the key to having a good time. No, that's not how it works! To get high in the right way is actually an art form. For maximum healthy enjoyment, one has to learn to do it right.

The doorbell rang downstairs and there was a murmur of voices. The deceased had obviously been a popular person, as more of his friends were turning up by the minute.

The back door leading from the kitchen into the garden opened and a bunch of people carrying candles and bowls of food came out. And, I shit you not, there was the weirdo of Canning

Town, walking slowly in front of everybody else, in his white suit and sporting his ridiculous eighties haircut!

Chapter 15

Standing in my dark room, surrounded in gloom, I looked breathlessly down into the garden, where the faces of the men and women shone in the light of candles, like in a particularly dark and spooky Bauhaus cinema movie. And upstairs, I was in a Harry Potter movie, eavesdropping from the shadows...

There was a lot going on. Some of the guys carried the kitchen table out, while women walked back and forth with food, plates and cups. It seemed the whole parish was here, for there were about twenty people gathered below me. The weirdo in the white suit had brought a teapot with him and positioned it carefully in the centre of the table. Everyone looked very serious.

As soon as the table was ready, everybody went back inside, the door was closed, and the sound of voices speaking quietly drifted up through the floorboards from the room below. The candles on the table stayed lit. I opened my door a bit. It was dark, and nobody would notice me on the small landing that divided my room from Rahima's room and the bathroom. I sat on the landing floor and listened to the voices below. I felt very tense, not only about the failure of our business plan and the argument it had led to, but also, I must admit, about Nansen and Askolds. The overall atmosphere in the house at the moment was so strange that no way could I go to sleep now.

Downstairs, several people spoke simultaneously and incomprehensibly. But then everybody became quiet, and the unexpected silence was filled with the sound of a guitar and someone singing about Jesus. The song was started by just one singer, but soon everybody joined in and the sound grew larger, into a hymn. There is a musical term, 'stadium rock', which implies songs with a simple melodic and rhythmic structure and memorable choruses – like 'Wind of change' by The Scorpions. They trigger an urge to light up your lighter and sway from left to right synchronously with Klaus Meine, if you know what I mean. The soloist downstairs didn't whistle like Klaus did, yet in the middle of the song there was a moment often exploited by rock bands – the instruments go quiet and the audience claps the rhythm with their hands and sings the chorus in unison. And here it was. *What an irony*, I thought to myself – one of the reasons I had come here in the first place was the wish to be on stage myself and make everybody clap along with *my* songs…

The song ended with hallelujahs and amens; then there was a brief silence.

Then I heard the weirdo start up.

"We are gathered here tonight to honour the memory of a friend and a trustworthy Christian. Darius is not among us anymore, but we wait impatiently to meet him again in the heavenly dwellings of the New Jerusalem!"

His voice still had that elongated, slightly pained expression we sometimes get to hear in a Christmas or Easter sermon. He went on to list the virtues of the said Darius, as well as his friends and children in Lithuania who would never forget him. God had created him, then God had taken him, ashes to ashes, yet in our hearts he would stay forever.

"Amen," agreed everybody.

There was a slight pause.

Then the preacher's voice suddenly lost its lilting, feminine tone and, with the speed of light, the funeral address turned in a direction I hadn't been expecting. Was the death of Darius an unfortunate coincidence? Was he just lost in the aimless hurricane of mundane life? Had his death just been a twist of fate? No! The weirdo exclaimed, and everybody hummed in agreement.

"We know everything is now set for the last event. We don't have to feel desperate or sad about the fact that Darius is not among us in the flesh anymore. Why should we? He is already in a place much better than this, and is working together with the greatest carpenter in the world to finish off the city of light where we are all going to be together, forever!"

Amens, hallelujahs and cries of 'yes, yes!' followed.

The best carpenter in the world? Jesus was a carpenter, wasn't he? He had learnt the trade from Joseph. I listened closely again. The voice of the speaker had changed once more – now it held rolling thunder, and if someone had had to write down what he said in pictograms there would have been plenty of lightning bolts, dark clouds and tornadoes. Now he was going on about the four horsemen coming from afar and bringing pain and torture as never seen before. The earth itself would contract in suffering. All the governments in the world were corrupted gangs of thieves and possessed by the Evil One. The world had been overcome by the worst form of genocide – abortion – and homosexuals were trying to turn every town in the world into Sodom and Gomorrah. That would fulfil the prophecy that says that on the Judgement Day all cities will be thrown into fire, and sinful souls will die their last and permanent death.

"Yeess!" everyone yelled.

The eulogy had moved uncontrollably in a new direction. I didn't quite get the next part, but the main idea was that when Jesus came back, his eyes shining in the darkness like searchlights sweeping the sky, a double edged sword would be coming out of his mouth[30], with which he would scythe to his left and right without pity. The locusts from the Book of Revelation were actually helicopters spreading napalm over the earth, and the soldiers of Satan would receive firearms from the warehouses in the Pentagon. Thanks to experiments on human genomes and DNA, the members of the secret government of the world would be turned into monsters, and everywhere there would be nothing but desperation and grinding of teeth.

Like everybody else with an interest in Iron Maiden, I too had read the Revelation of John, yet understanding it literally had never crossed my mind before.

"And then the sun will die; it will turn black and terrifying, and crush the earth, for the Lord will not hold it in the sky anymore. It will be a horrible, horrible end!"

It sounded like trouble, certainly. But then he offered a ray of light and hope.

"The Lord has said: the hour is nigh when the mundane world will crash into hellish flame and noise, but the true believers will be lifted up on the wings of their love. Our sinful bodies will evanesce in the heavenly rain, as if dissolved by an acid, and our spiritual bodies will become free, and the wings of

---

[30]Revelation 19:15.

love will make us similar to angels. Hallelujah! Thank you, Jesus!"

The excitement downstairs knew no boundaries. Like a real rock star, the man knew how to manipulate his audience. His voice cut through the noise like the blade of a knife.

"The storms will break out and the darkness of the dead sun will be only illuminated by the hellish flames and sparks flying up from the burning bodies of sinners! The Beast will scream madly and bite the spear that went through his trunk, but in vain!' ('Halleluiah! Amen!' shouted his public). 'But us – we will glide high above, easy and trembling with joy, higher than every teeth-grinding sinner and follower of Satan, and even higher, above us – oh, absolutely unwillingly, my friends, do these tears of joy come to my eyes, and love takes over the whole of me – above us, my friends, shining golden rays of light, the New Jerusalem will lower itself down from heavens!"

I stretched my legs out on the carpet in the dark. As far as I could gather, the preacher was on about what they call the Rapture. This is the theory that on Doomsday the true believers will experience an ecstasy that will lift them upwards above the ground, where they will meet the souls of those deceased righteous ones, while all sinners will be sliced and diced ad interim.

"Look around!" The weirdo exclaimed. I imagined him making a wide circle with his hand. "The Lord is sending signs to the believers, and the signs speak incontrovertibly. The Holy Spirit speaks! It speaks to us, let it speak! Hallelujah, *rahamarantabarakaradaramatara! Guramangha raga rutaka!*"

Now this was something I had never heard before. Of course, I cannot guarantee that these were exactly the words the preacher said, or that the spelling is right, but at least something pretty damn close to it. I didn't know it at the time, but he was speaking in tongues. Later, Valdas explained it to me. There are people out there who think that the Holy Spirit enters the physical bodies of praying individuals and speaks with their mouths. If he makes the person speak in a language the speaker does not understand, but some others do because they know the language, it is called xenolalia. As an example, let's imagine me meeting the President of Iceland (not the frozen ready meals shop, but country), Ólafur Ragnar Grímsson, and speaking to him in Icelandic, a language that is only spoken in Iceland: if I wouldn't understand a single word of what I was saying, whereas he would understand me perfectly – that would be xenolalia. However, in real life things are usually much simpler. People usually utter something no one understands and that, my friends, is called glossolalia. If I visited President Grímsson again and this time around I said something neither I, nor he, nor anybody else could make sense of, that would be glossolalia.

Right now there was a real orgy of glossolalia taking place downstairs. It sounded as if everybody was joining in. I could hear female voices making barking sounds and men weeping like babies. Once in a while my ear caught some more comprehensible vocalisations, like 'amen', 'hallelujah' or 'Jesus!' with Lithuanian or English pronunciation. '*Ak Jezau, Jezau, Dieve gailestingase*[1] "In the name of the Father, and of the Son, and of the Holy Spirit!' The event was truly emotional and deeply felt, beyond any doubt.

The prayer finished with a song, exactly as it had started. After that, emotions settled down a little and the casual socialising recommenced, judging by the sounds of voices and cutlery touching plates and tea cups. Everybody seemed to be moving outside into the garden. I stood up and peeped downstairs. The table was adorned with candles and everybody was standing around chewing sandwiches and drinking tea or juice. There were also bowls full of fruit and cookies. The weirdo, of course, stood at the end of the table and had a flock of ladies around him. Say what you will, there are parallels between religion and rock music.

I went to bed and lay without moving for a long time, staring at the dark ceiling. Eventually, my thoughts started to dissolve into each other and I fell asleep, tired from the long day. Downstairs somebody laughed and fragments of conversations drifted into my ears, entering my dreams. The quality of sleep I enjoyed that night could be called mediocre at best. In the middle of the night, an especially noisy bunch woke me up whilst saying their goodbyes. The whole night my brain squirmed inside its casing, mixing up images of the Armageddon, with its battle copters, people turned into monsters via DNA manipulation,

---

[1] Oh Jesus, Jesus, merciful God. *(Lithuanian)*

with seething bottles of cannamilk – and in the middle of it all, Emil and his balding Berliners in their leather caps, performing dance moves like waves on the sea.

When I finally woke up the next morning, the house was silent. The Lithuanians had left, presumably for another sermon, and Rahima wasn't back yet. Apparently she had celebrated the weekend at somebody else's. I phoned Nansen and found out that he and Askolds were in the tent, home and dry, but couldn't remember how they had got there. Splendid, everybody was where they belonged, so the previous night hadn't turned out too badly in the end – apart from our business plan falling through, that is.

Chapter 16

Whatever stormy weather raged in the Christian camp, the rest of London was breathing normally, or at least so it seemed. I visited Nansen a couple of times and brought him a portable gas cooker with an aluminium saucepan as a present. Askolds had moved into tent accommodation as well because Stu had it in his mind that there was a strong link between him and us and had kicked the poor guy out of the squat.

Once I spent a night with them, enjoying the natural wonders of the English forest. We drank a bottle of Famous Grouse with ginger ale mixers, grilled sausages on the open fire, made some tea on the camping cooker and discussed King Crimson versus Robert Fripp going solo. I wondered why Askolds was still wearing a suit, though, sitting in the forest before an open fire. Since jacket potatoes roasted in ash and coal[31] was the staple food of the camp, the suit looked considerably worse than when I met him for the first time.

"I have no other clothes but suits," Askolds said, sticking his chin forward belligerently. All he had brought to England with him was a spare suit, a laptop, a pair of socks and undies, and his university certificate. For, lo and behold, Askolds held a bachelor's degree in Economics from the University of Latvia. He wasn't going to labour on a building site or work for peanuts as a waiter. His aim was to sit in an excitingly expensive fake leather chair behind a desk in a bank, or its equivalent. His dream was to become a bank cashier, or even a manager, and he concentrated solely on that. He had been sending his CVs and portfolios to every possible place for four months now, yet without any favourable outcome. During those four months he

---

[31] Traditional Latvian camping snack. It is to us as BBQ is to Aussies.

had had only one job interview, but it had been unsuccessful. The money had run out, and he didn't want to ask his parents for more since they had only agreed to send money for a ticket back home. Yet Askolds didn't back down. The opportunity to camp in the forest near London allowed him to survive there longer. He'd spend his mornings reading the *Financial Times* in the village library and go into central London or Docklands every second day, looking for an office job. Unfortunately, his funds for CV printing at internet cafés had run out and, quite out of character, Nansen was now supporting him, rather than being supported himself.

Naturally, such an anomaly could not carry on for too long, and one day Nansen confronted Askolds. I don't know exactly what was said, but the last time I saw Askolds was on a damn cold and drippy late afternoon when I was visiting them with another bottle of Famous Grouse. There was a nasty drizzle in the air. The chilling wind from the wide open field on the verge of the forest penetrated all the way to my bone marrow, and the clouds made it feel like early evening. I was about halfway between the train station and the camp when I noticed Askolds sitting on a fallen trunk by the path, sheltering beneath the massive canopy of a linden tree. The foliage obviously wasn't enough, as he also had the collar of his suit jacket up and an umbrella with a broken spike in his hand. Surprised, I stopped.

"Hi!" I said.

He returned the greeting without enthusiasm.

"What are you doing here? Where's Nansen?"

"We had an argument." Despite the situation, Askolds seemed to be as aloof as usual, as though he was above all regular folk. "I live in my own camp now."

"Oh." I couldn't think of anything more appropriate to say in response.

The rain drops quietly hit the umbrella and bounced back on the young green leaves of stinging nettles. Askolds exuded such dignity and loneliness in his solitude. Eventually, I nodded and trotted further through the drizzling rain towards the tent. There, guests were allowed to wrap their feet in Nansen's warm sleeping bag and share the tea boiling in the saucepan on the camping cooker. Hot tea with whisky was exactly what was needed right now.

Nansen described the main reasons behind their split clearly and succinctly.

"He pissed me off entirely. Let him build his office under a bush, I don't give a fuck."

So we washed down some giggle juice and spent a very pleasant evening discussing different aspects of Jim Morrison's poetry. Sometimes an intellectual conversation can be unbelievably satisfying and fulfilling.

Living in a tent has its ups and downs. On one hand, the sounds of the surrounding world make you feel one with nature. On the other, if you live there long enough, nylon's propensity to retain condensation becomes a considerable irritant. It seems all the bad smells enter the fabric of your dwelling and decide to never leave, regardless of how much you aerate the place. Sleeping bags soak up odours of the flesh, and the space between the walls of the tent and its tarp gets claimed as *Lebensraum*[1] by an astonishing array of insects. In no time at all, they also conquer the inside.

That night I had my harshest eco-tramp experience to date, and it was all to do with cigarette butts. Parsimoniously, Nansen would save all the leftovers of his roll-ups, as well as the dog-ends he found around the local supermarket entrance (people tend to throw away longer dog-ends if they have to enter a building and they also tend to stay dry for longer when under a roof). All these he kept in his belt bag. In the dark dampness of the bag the tobacco brewed and fermented like a stew made of dirty socks, especially when the dampness of true English weather kicked in. Even the portable cooker couldn't help – it simply wasn't powerful enough to dry all the clothes, the tent, the sleeping bag, boots, socks, food items and Nansen's collection of dog-ends. And when you boil your tea inside a tent, in a saucepan with no lid, the vapour makes things even worse.

That night only neat whisky and wisdom of ancestors saved Nansen's tent from being filled with digestive discharge. You see, it was like this: we took our boots off, exposing to the already less than fragrant air our builders' socks, which typically let you know the tradesmen are in the building long before you actually get to see one. We threw some PG Tips teabags into the

---

[1] Living space. *(German)* Nazi connotations intended.

saucepan and wrapped our feet in the sleeping bag. Our steel-toe boots had to be kept inside the tent, because of the rain. As you can imagine, the atmosphere in the little dwelling grew increasingly picante.

And at that moment – I'd like to make a dramatic pause here, to escalate the narrative, so, everybody: take a deep breath and hold it – at that moment, I say, NANSEN OPENED HIS BELT BAG TO MAKE A ROLL-UP.

Umph-grrrrr.

My grey-haired granddad, bless him, taught me two things one can use in order not to waste low-quality moonshine: first, you can smell your own armpit after your first shot; second, you can blow your cheeks out and knock back one more as quickly as possible. The trick is that the second shot usually seems to be so revolting it completely neutralises the first, thus establishing an ideal equilibrium of positively and negatively charged particles in the organism.

I followed the wisdom of my ancestors. I blew my cheeks till it hurt and rushed down my throat some Famous Grouse, whose mission was to keep everything where it was right now, and not to let it move! It helped.

Now you see what an ancient family tradition can be capable of. We opened the door a little and let some fresh air in. Finally, Nansen zipped his bag up and we were all right again.

After all, a guest has no moral right to criticise the premises that welcome him.

About Askolds, though, I haven't heard much since then. Sometimes I think he might have admitted defeat and either become a road sweeper or returned to Latvia, where the Latvian certificate of higher education is valuated more highly than in the UK. Yet at other times, if I have had one drink too many and feel nostalgia engulfing my soul, as a second possibility, I imagine him wandering the forests and parks of Greater London, still in his suit and tie, laptop bag over the shoulder and feeding himself on sorrels and pine shoots. All in all, the winters in England are quite mild. But if that is the case, Nansen would have met him sooner or later. As a third possibility, we might assume he got his dream job and is smoking a fat cigar right now, standing on the balcony of his office and critically comparing his

Lamborghini against a colleague's Porsche. Which I truly wish him from the bottom of my heart.

The work on our *stroika* in Baker Street was already finished. At the end of the week, I received a call from the agency informing me that from the next week I would be working on a new site on Pall Mall. Yes, not far from Buckingham Palace, in an area so posh even public toilets have coats of arms on them. And – hooray – they were also giving me half a day of overtime that Saturday and Sunday! Work at the weekend means an eight-to-one shift for which you get a full day's pay (actually the customer is paying way more than that, but the agents greedily rake most of that money into their own pockets). I had a parting chat with everybody on the site, saved the phone numbers of a couple of people that might help with jobs in the future and spent the last two days in complete relaxation, mostly chatting with Rob about reggae, Rastafarianism and life in Jamaica. There was no point doing much on my last days anyway as the money wouldn't change. The Lithuanians finished on Friday, but I still had both Saturday and Sunday to spend on the site. On Sunday, I had a long and relaxing tea break at nine, at the end of which we shared a spliff with Rob and our main manager Janusz. Around eleven, I finally got my ass in the gear, grabbed my carpenter's chest on wheels and left for home two hours early. There was nothing to do anyway.

I arrived home after twelve. There was a new job to start the next day, so I felt it would be a good idea to sort out and clean all my tools and then probably have a go at a new computer game. I had to be prepared for tomorrow, with a clear head and well rested.

The activities of the Lithuanians had been depressingly intense lately and made me feel uneasy; hence, it was a relief that none of them was home at the moment. I pulled my carpenter's chest out into the garden, spread all my tools on the grass, tightened up some screws here or there, sharpened a couple of chisels and neatly sorted all my drill bits in their leather case. Usually, in the course of work, the drill bits got hopelessly mixed up and some of the auger bits would wander from their case and end up amongst the translucent, amber handles of Faithfull chisels. I even turned the chest upside down to get rid of the annoying sawdust and plasterboard debris at the bottom.

A light breeze across the garden gently shook the dark branches of our old apple tree, its leaves dusty from the urban air. It wasn't cold but the wind brought my skin up in goose bumps. To enjoy such a silent afternoon fully, a warm jacket and a Drum roll-up were required, I felt.

When I entered the kitchen the sound of the wind ceased and dead silence surrounded me. Sometimes being alone at home is highly enjoyable. Peace and relaxation. Slowly, I rolled up my smoke, then pecked around the cooker for the matches, but couldn't find them. Taking my time, I opened the drawers one by one, until – behold – I found a crushed matchbox in one of them, amongst some rusty forks, breadcrumbs and an old bottle opener, all resting beside the titmag Agris had given the Krasko brothers before he left. The thing was still curled up in a roll like a glossy pipe. They must have been too shy to declare that on the border, I told myself, grinning. Interestingly enough, I hadn't looked at the issue myself. I had left for Latvia myself soon after it arrived, and had completely forgotten about it upon my return. I pulled the magazine out. Impressive. I turned the first page over. Pretty face, no doubt, but the blue veins on breasts stretched to their limits by implants destroyed the good impression. *Hmmm, how about a cup of coffee and a relaxing titmag session?* Nothing can be crueller to your cardiology and yet more enjoyable than coffee with a strong roll-up. A thorough kick to the heart. After such a doping, I would sort all the tools out much quicker and then play Grand Theft Auto with much sharper senses. And I also had an appropriate read for my coffee break.

Once the plan was settled, my first step was to put the kettle on – but it had disappeared. I looked around and soon discovered some other things had gone missing as well – the tin opener, the big shiny pan me and Nansen had used for the cannamilk, and all the cups I remembered the Lithuanians had brought with them when they moved in. I noticed that our red plastic dish dryer was almost empty, containing only my favourite Beano plate and Rahima's football mug. Then I saw that the iron was gone from the living room, where it normally stood in the corner by the telly. That too belonged to the Lithuanians. A dark thought grew in my brain; I dropped the magazine on the low table by the TV in the living room and knocked on the door to the room shared by Tall Stan and Short Stan. No reply. I opened the door.

The room was empty. Well, I mean, the original furniture was still there, but all the clothes, books, DVDs and tools were gone. The same applied to the other room, shared by Rimantas and Valdas. *The buggers had just left without saying anything! Had everybody deserted me?* Recently there had been a lot of talk about the end of the world, so it felt rather eerie, to be honest. I ran upstairs and burst into Rahima's room.

"Are you completely fucking out of your mind?" Rahima retorted, lifting her face, puffy from sleep, from the pillow. The blanket slid off her shoulders, revealing tempting curves.

"Where are the Lithuanians?"

"I don't know no Lithuanians," she hissed and pulled the blanket up to her nose. "Go away! Why, WHY is all this shit always arranged so as to fucking piss me off? You're doing it all deliberately, aren't you – you're just pissing me off because you enjoy it, don't you? Is the whole universe against me, or is it just you idiots?"

Well, at least Rahima was where she was supposed to be and the same as always. I shut the door and went downstairs again. The Lithuanian chippies had definitely gone, even though they must have been there in the morning – I remembered using the kettle before I went to work, and the hallway had been full of their shoes and boots. Now, all the steel toes, sneakers and flip-flops were gone.

Calls to their mobiles produced nothing. Their numbers were 'currently unavailable'. *Could they be in some specific church meeting, where everybody had to turn up with a kettle and all their other possessions, including ironing boards and flip-flops?* It was an absolute mystery. Admittedly, it was the thirteenth of May, even though a Sunday, not a Friday. Still – whattafuck? But then again their behaviour recently had been so weird, generally. I boiled the water for my coffee in the little pan we normally used to boil eggs in, sat down again and unrolled the glossy scroll of the titmag. Silicone. *There must be at least some natural models in the thing*, I thought to myself, and was about to turn another page when the doorbell rang. Reluctantly, I threw the magazine back on the magazine table and went for the door.

It was Nansen. He was standing on the threshold in very merry spirits, and his Jesus-like countenance shone with delight.

Again, it turned out, he had had an idea for how to become rich quickly and effortlessly.

"They kicked me out of my job," he exclaimed jubilantly as soon as I opened the door, "but it's all right! This time, I have something that will really blow your mind, man, and it will work as sure as a bank mortgage, and in big numbers!"

I suppressed a sigh and stepped aside to let him in. "I'm not superstitious, Nansen, but it seems to me today is not a good day to start anything. It's the thirteenth, you know. Your previous idea already cost us enough money and nerves."

"Don't you worry – it will be precise and legit this time around! Fuck cannamilk and the squatters – we're gonna brew hanka!"

God Almighty. The last thing I wanted to associate my name with was hanka – a heroin substitute made with poppies boiled in paint solvent, an old recipe of Soviet prison inmates and hippies. I wasn't going to make, sell or even keep that shit, I told Nansen right away. But he wasn't listening. Instead, he produced a Lidl bag out of his rucksack and triumphantly opened it before me.

Oh, my fucking days, I wanted to exclaim, but I kept my mouth shut so as not to excite him even more. Real poppies, at this time of the year! They were quite young and probably hadn't even any properly developed seeds inside the pods yet, but without any doubt they were *Papaverum somniferum. Where the heck had he found them?*

"Over my Maryjane field, where I picked the hemp first time around, there are some allotments, similar to those we had in Soviet times," Nansen told me, anticipating my question. "I got sick and tired of nicking vegetables from the supermarket all the time, so I browsed around for some. I checked out a couple of the greenhouses, and there you go! One of them is kept really warm with massive heaters inside. There are some poppies growing outside, but they haven't even started to blossom. The ones from inside the greenhouse have decent pods already, so we can grind them right away."

"Not here, mate. My neighbours won't get it, and neither will I. Besides, you don't have the solvent."

"No," he agreed, "but I'm gonna buy a bottle!"

"You need the old Soviet paint solvent number 646, remember? British solvents are based on different chemicals, I bet! This will end with a disaster worse than the chocolate faucet we induced in Stu's squat."

"I'm sure the main principle is the same." He was electrified at the thought of his plan. "There are a couple of guys on my old job who fancy buying some as soon as we make it. And if that goes well they know somebody who could take a big chunk!"

'Are you not afraid to get your snout broken in by the owners of the greenhouse?'

"Don't you worry, mate, they're not going to notice, I'm sure! It's not a fucking drug factory full of Colombians, you know. Must be some elderly lady growing poppies to seed her doughnuts. Can't we try it just once?"

There we went again. *What kind of karma is this that constantly leads this man to cannabis, poppies and other crap? And what kind of karma do I possess myself, to be in the same boat as him, a boat that is bound to land me either in prison or in an early grave, whichever happens to be first?* On the other hand, I had to admit, it could be quite interesting. I had never made or used hanka before. Yet I had had some conversations on the subject with the veterans, and that gave me a certain idea.

Which reminded me of something else.

"You don't have any dimedrol[32], do you? The guys always used to add dimedrol, I remember that clearly."

"Sure, I can get you dimedrol. The chaps who want to buy the hanka can also supply me with dimedrol. And I'll get the solvent too, don't you worry."

Oh, there was nothing to worry about, not at all. First, almost all of my flatmates had disappeared like a ship's crew in the Bermuda triangle; then I had been verbally abused by the last remaining member of the house; and then an ex-classmate insisted we should cook homemade heroin with the wrong solvent and dodgy dimedrol... no grounds to be stressed then.

'Nansen,' I protested, 'I don't want to be involved in any of this. Your cannamilk had to be poured down the toilet because it went off in a couple of days. Now where am I supposed to keep

---

[32] Also known as Diphenhydramine in the UK. It is a fairly widespread antihistamine and sedative.

your hanka? It's a form of heroin. You know that. People won't treat it quite as light-heartedly as cannabis. Hanka is a serious business – it gets delivered through a needle!'

Nansen spread his arms wide, as though surrendering.

"OK, OK, I understand you're scared. At least let me put the pods under your bed till tomorrow so they can dry. Tomorrow I'll get them out of your house. Promise."

With the darkest of thoughts and mistrust in my heart, I allowed Nansen to spread the poppies under my bed on an old *Metro* newspaper, and then off he went. He promised to pop in the next day, and bring some dimedrol.

Chapter 17

Literally three minutes after Nansen left, Rahima came downstairs. She spent the next couple of hours cooking, so my innate shyness made me to put the titmag aside and turn to the PlayStation. She left when it was almost dark and soon thereafter I had another visitor – the key turned in the keyhole and Valdas stormed in with Stolichnaya and gherkins and marinated mushrooms, a jar of each. Already quite pissed, he insisted on me taking a part in the banquet, and I could not resist. Firstly, it was an equivalent to Grand Theft Auto in itself, and secondly, I was keen to find out where everybody was and what had happened.

Valdas explained everything straight away.

"Tomorrow is the fourteenth of May," he told me as he fished out two tea cups from among the dirty plates in the sink so we would have something to pour the vodka into. "Tomorrow is the end of the world."

I am inclined to hope that no muscle moved on my poker face, since Valdas carried on, casually busying himself with plates, cups and jars on the magazine table in the living room. We sat ourselves down on the big sofa. Carefully, I asked for further info.

"In 1633, Irish Archbishop James Ussher counted the genealogies of all the people mentioned in the Bible and calculated that the world was created on the twenty-third of October in the year 4004 before Christ. Precisely then. Right now it is May in the year 2001, so the world and the rest of the universe is now roughly six-thousand years old. God created the universe in six days and rested on the seventh. The Bible says that a thousand years for a man is one day for God. So, the world was destined to exist for six-thousand years, and the six days of God are almost over. We also believe that the word of the

Saviour had to be preached for two-thousand years, and that is also fulfilled now, in the year 2001."

Valdas poured some vodka into a teacup with sentimental roses on it and handed it to me. We downed the drink and helped ourselves to gherkin zakuska – the best way of taking the edge off after you just had a proper shot. I asked him to continue. After a hiccup, continue he did.

"Pardon me. In the Bible, somebody asks Jesus when the end of the world will come. He answers that nobody knows, yet look at the olive tree: when it sprouts its leaves, you shall know that the summer is near. Which means that you shall see certain signs that will indicate that the end is nigh. That olive tree stands for the house of Israel. You see, it is written that one generation after Israel has its house back, the prophecies will be fulfilled and Jesus will return to earth. Israel became an independent country on the fourteenth of May 1948. Tomorrow, it will be Israeli Independence Day. That makes it fifty-three years, absolutely enough to fulfil the prophecy about one generation." He gave me a serious, oddly confidential look. "Actually, no one can really tell how much time a biblical generation really is, which makes it difficult to work the exact date out. Only the chosen ones know."

I couldn't resist the temptation to ask the obvious question. "So are you the chosen ones?"

It seemed so self-evident to him that he just shrugged his shoulders. "Yep. At least Doctor Butt is. He had a revelation, where God's angels explained everything. The end of the world is tomorrow, because tomorrow is Israeli Independence Day and two-thousand years since the birth of the Saviour."

"So where is everybody? Where is your stuff?"

"In the church. Everything and everyone."

I recalled that they had mentioned a temple somewhere in East London before now. Valdas took a deep breath, looked at the ceiling and flinched painfully.

"We believe in one thing – tomorrow's the day. Get it? Mundane stuff has no meaning or value anymore. Everything is in the storage room by the church, to get it out of our way. Everybody is spending their time in prayer now, to strengthen themselves. It's just me, the wicked sinner and a weakling, who still has doubts in his heart. I know we must be strong, but still there is a worm of doubt in me, planted there by Satan, I guess. I am still contemplating and trying to understand what I have done. Have I done enough to rectify my sins? Will I be forgiven? That's why I need someone to explain myself to. I want to confess my sins to you. I can't talk to my lot about this, and there isn't enough time to find an ordained minister. If you are baptised, that should be enough – you could give me your answer and accept my confession. As a brother, you understand?"

I glanced at the rolled-up titmag on the table under his elbow but kept my silence. Let him who hasn't sinned be the first to cast the stone, or whatever the saying is…

My companion clearly needed to talk to somebody.

"No, don't object," he interrupted before I could reply, wagging his finger at me, "I know very well that God has a special plan for every one of us. But let me tell you first why I am such a sinner. Now, read this first."

He took an old issue of *Metro* out of the inner pocket of his jacket and threw it across the table. The poor newspaper had suffered a lot in the extreme environment of the *stroika* and was all white from plasterboard dust. One corner of it had been exposed to a crushed tomato, judging by the yellowish stain with some seeds stuck to it. Right below the stain there was an article that made my guts shrink inside. Here's the gist.

Canning Town Basement Body is Lithuanian

A body found several months ago in the basement of a house in Canning Town has been identified as Mr Darius Maisiulis, from Stratford.

Mr Maisiulis, 46, worked illegally in one of the East London building companies.

Evidence suggests he was killed by a sharp object hitting his temple. The body was disposed of in the freshly laid concrete floor of a Canning Town property basement.

Scotland Yard has confirmed that the state police of Lithuania have joined the investigation.

Could it be the same house? Transfixed, I stared at the newspaper. There were no photos by the article that could help me find out whether it was the same place where I had practised shuttering carpentry for the first time in my life. On the other

149

hand – *how many basements with bodies in the floor could there be in Canning Town?*

"Nobody killed him," Valdas murmured, and pushed my refilled teacup under my nose.

I swallowed the vodka down in one go.

Valdas fixed me with a steady look. "I was there when Darius died. That's the thing."

I felt like having another shot right away, but restrained myself. Keep calm, I ordered myself. Yet the leg sticking out of the concrete appeared before my mind's eye as vivid and real as it had been back then. Suddenly, the drink irritated my throat and I coughed.

"So," I asked after a moment's pause, "you knew this guy?"

"Hah, did I know him? Of course I did, since way back in Lithuania. Great guy, Darius was, an orphan and a widower. He taught me a lot of things about life, about God… Me and him were like this," he added, spreading the fingers of both his hands wide, and then interlocking them like cogwheels. "It was him who convinced me to leave Lithuania and come to work here. Come to London, he said, and spread the Gospel among our people abroad. They are having a hard time. Satan tempts them with big incomes…"

He bit into a crunchy gherkin and then licked the marinade off his fingers.

"The job was great. We were working for a man of God. Practically all the profit we made for the company went into church activities and evangelical crusades organised in the name of the Lord by Doctor Butt. I mean the profit outside our wages, of course. The wages were actually quite good; we paid the tithe, obviously, but it was still all right. The profit went towards things God loves – like a new synthesiser for the church, free booklets and so on."

Something puzzled me. "So what sort of job were you doing?"

"What do you mean, what sort? Construction, of course. Doctor Butt would buy an old house and we refurbished it in the name of God. He is our shepherd, and a pastor, and general manager at the same time. In the beginning, he even did all the deliveries with the van, all by himself. We used to say – it is not appropriate for a priest to deliver sacks of cement, but he just replies that work is not a sin, it is an honour. What a man! And the further it went, the better. When I first came to work, Doctor Butt had only one house, where four guys from our church were doing the refurbishment. Over the next three years, we grew into a proper company. Everybody did their best to move things forward and in a while we even had some subcontractors. That's right; we even had a black geezer, who got involved with all his family. I mean, before God we're all equal – I don't mind Africans. And as long as I knew him, he never missed a Sunday sermon. Ever. Now that's what I call faith!"

A black geezer with the whole family. I splashed some more vodka into the cup and gulped it down. Valdas followed suit, then we took a gherkin each.

"Yeah… everything was going on so well," Valdas resumed. "But as you know calamities never advertise themselves beforehand. We Lithuanians were working all together on a site in Canada Water. Our subcontractor had a site in Canning Town.' He tapped the newspaper with his index finger. 'I know that place well. It was actually us who started the demolition work there, but then Doctor Butt moved us to the Canada Water site, so the African geezer carried on by himself with some mercenaries."

I swallowed a marinated mushroom from the jar. "Listen, Valdas, I also–"

He interrupted me, imperatively shaking a gherkin at me. "Never hire a mercenary! All they care about is money. They have no God in their hearts! I heard later on that they had a brickie who was a total arse, couldn't arrange even a few rows of bricks in a straight line. But that's not the point."

All I could do now was utter a squeak of agreement.

"And so, me and Darius were both working in Canada Water. We had done almost all of it. In some rooms, we even had the furniture in already. There was some snagging to be done and a marble worktop to be fixed in the kitchen, that's all. It was a big thing, that worktop. It was Friday night and everything else was done, so the other guys went home. It was only me and Darius who were left. The delivery man was running late, so Doctor Butt phoned us up and told to wait for the delivery. So we did. Doctor Butt wanted us to get it done that same day since we were behind the schedule and the customer was coming to look at our progress the next morning. I told him it wouldn't be that quick if there were only two of us."

Valdas looked at me and I saw that his eyes were wet. He covered his forehead with both hands.

"Doctor Butt himself arrived to help us. He said he happened to be in the area doing some church business. We fixed the worktop on the trolley, tied it with ropes – all was OK, you know... the kitchen was on the first floor, up some winding stairs. It was a terribly awkward task. We decided to lift the worktop up with ropes and then along the circular landing. Darius held it from below while the priest and I pulled it up. A heavy bastard, I'm telling you, almost three square metres of granite... then one rope snapped and the whole sheet moved sideways. It didn't fall, of course, as it was secured with three other ropes – but yeah, it lurched sideways and hit Darius right in the temple."

Valdas sat quietly for a moment, catching his breath. I was too stunned by his story to move or speak. I could envisage the dead body of the builder right there in front of me, with his horribly smashed skull. And then Weirdo, with his eighties haircut – by now I had no doubt it was him – reciting a prayer over a pool of blood that grew larger and larger...

"Darius died on the spot," Valdas continued. 'We recited a prayer. I wanted to call an ambulance, but Doctor Butt told me not to. He was quite right. It was obvious, even to me who is not a medic, that Darius's soul had departed for a better place. The Lord sows and reaps as he likes.'

I cleared my throat. "But you called an emergency number anyway, right?"

Valdas didn't say a word for at least a minute. The air above the crumpled issue of *Metro* grew thicker.

"I am just an average person, a mediocre sinner, like most people are... Doctor Butt said it was better if we didn't tell anybody. People would just become unnecessarily curious and they would start to criticise our work – the work of the church, I mean. There were at least ten people working for the company who had no official papers whatsoever. They would deport every single one of us. More than that, we never paid too much attention to all that English Health and Safety stuff. No one had ever worn a helmet or a high viz vest on our sites... Darius always wore sneakers and shorts at work." (So that explained the naked leg I had seen, I realised). "That damn worktop! I know we could have done it safer, but we were in a rush, you see. In fact, everything we did for that company was done like that. We always rely on God to keep us safe, and so far, he always had. Until the day when that rope snapped... truly, what a stupid death. Sometimes I think – if only we had taken more care, he'd be alive now," Valdas concluded with a sigh.

I couldn't think of a subtler way to find out what I wanted to know, so I just spat my question out damn straight. "What did you do with the corpse?"

"Er... thanks be to God, the floor was still covered in dustsheets, so we left no marks. We simply fitted the worktop and then changed the dustsheets. We wrapped Darius in sheets and put new sheets down everywhere. Oh, what a wicked, wicked sinner I am – Willis, just tell me, did I do the right thing?"

"Wait, what did you do at the end?"

"We wrapped him in the sheets and tied a plastic rubbish bag on his head, then stuck him in the bedroom wardrobe. Doctor Butt said that now everything was in the hands of the Lord."

"You didn't leave the body in the wardrobe, did you?"

Valdas shook his head and with a pained expression splashed the last of the vodka into our cups. He held the bottle over the second cup for a moment, his hand shaking, in a habitual manly gesture to make sure the last drop was gone, and then rolled the bottle under the sofa. We clinked glasses.

"Surely not," he replied at last. "When I came to work the following Monday, there was no trace of Darius's body, no trace at all of what happened. The worktop was all done and the sink hole cut and all plumbed up... Eeeeer... what a sinner, what a sinner... I told everybody Darius had had to return to Vilnius for a family emergency. I said he told me his daughter was sick. White lies, hey... but it was legit this time, I know. God definitely likes it more when we can continue as a church, and spread the Gospel. Back then we had the plan to organise an evangelising trip to Venezuela, as missionaries, and we had even started to save up money for it, but then Doctor Butt had his revelation and it turned out that we couldn't manage such a trip in such a short time, so decided to concentrate on more local areas. And you know what? It was a good idea to stay. Here in

London, there is so much to do and so many souls to be saved. The Venezuela project would have demanded at least a couple of years, but there simply isn't that much time left in the universe. God does not play dice."

"So where did the body end up then?"

Valdas nodded at the newspaper. "On the Canning Town site."

"How did it get there?"

The Lithuanian shrugged his shoulders. "I presume Doctor Butt transported him there. I thought it was better if I didn't know too much, understand? If I knew, Satan would be able to pull my tongue and the words would slip out. Now, they have found him anyway. And I was praying day and night, for Darius, for myself, for Doctor Butt… the way he took Darius – that was a sign to us to end the business. Since then, we've been wandering around other people's building sites, not ours."

The tears finally spilt out and ran down the workman's stubbly cheeks. He grasped the edge of the sofa with both hands and started rocking backwards and forwards.

"I prayed to the Lord with all my soul! God moves in mysterious ways. If He wanted to take Darius's soul, that was up to Him; I had nothing to say about that, because it is a sin to object to God's will! I prayed for a sign from the Lord that he would let me understand that we did the right thing when it all happened. I'm scared! Doctor Butt said the Lord had taken good care of it, that everything would be OK, and no one would ever find out. But they did! It must have been an intervention from Satan. I only wish I knew how on earth the police found out! I've got the feeling that some sneaky bastard found out about it somehow and snitched on us. Oh, if only I could meet that misbegotten piece of shit!"

This last outburst robbed Valdas of his last strength and he collapsed in a corner of the sofa, sobbing quietly. I felt he was going to pass out soon.

Unfortunately, the vodka was finished. I stood up and walked across the room to our big French window and opened it fully. If you listened closely, over the usual urban humming above the gardens and streets of Leyton, you could hear the peace and quiet in the darkness. Darius Maisiulis wasn't here anymore, not on this sinful earth anyway, and I had helped build a place of rest for him. Never again would Darius swear loudly while carrying heavy bricks on a scaffold; never again would he bare his teeth while drilling into a concrete wall with a drill geared in the hammering mode... Even though I had never met him personally, there was a feeling we might have had something in common. I suppose our spiritual bond was sanctified by the blood we had spilt occasionally at work when cutting our hands deep with saw blades; with the sweat that soaked our dusty T-shirts; and with the bone-breaking tiredness we always took home with us after work. Besides – and this was rather unnerving – but the chances were that I would leave this world in a similar manner myself someday. Even on a well-maintained building site, dangers lurk everywhere.

"'Willis?" Valdas squeaked weakly from his corner.

"What?"

"Will you absolve my sins? I have doubted my choices, and doubted God's will... I did not have enough courage to say 'Let the things happen in a way the Lord wants them to happen, and if You have decided to take Darius's soul, then do so and let me praise You in my heart and in my prayer...' I was weak and sinful, oh Lord..."

His already quiet voice was diminishing in strength with every syllable. I stared at the black emptiness of our garden and felt as if my soul was being swept empty by a sweeping gang with brooms and hoovers. Strangely enough, there were no emotions, no reaction, nothing apart from thought-paralysing sadness. The sadness took control over me and said, "Go to sleep, moron, tomorrow there'll be a new day and new problems. As soon as you step in fresh shit, you forget the old one. So don't worry, be happy."

I turned around and sat back on the sofa. "Yes, Valdas, I absolve all your sins. Completely."

The Lithuanian nodded, either in agreement or with thanks, then his head sunk lower and he rolled over on one side, lovingly cuddling the armrest of the sofa, and fell asleep. I picked up the titmag and went upstairs. Apocalypse or not, I didn't like the idea of such literature lying around just like that. Our conversation had left me feeling somewhat nervous.

Yet that wasn't the end of surprises that day. Oh, no.

I sat on the bed and to take the edge off, opened the magazine at random. In the light of the bedside lamp, looking up at me from the glossy page was no one else but Rahima. It was her all right, without a shadow of a doubt, though perhaps a few years younger than we knew her now, and performing under the idiotic nickname Magnolia's Flower XXX. Open-mouthed, I flipped back to the beginning of the picture series. Initially, she was wearing a tracksuit and underwear, but with every page, there was less and less of it. There was a considerable number of photos of her in the nude, both from the front and, pardon me, from the rear as well. There was nothing hardcore about this session – it was simply a voluptuous babe with an enviable bust working out in a gym. Particularly nice was a shot of her wearing only her knickers and exercising on a treadmill. Her hair was tied up in a knot at the back and her face looked so innocent and sweet, yet very serious at the same time, eyes looking upwards as though in the grip of a spiritual experience, and bust sticking out in all its natural unaltered glory. Knowing her a little bit, I understood her choice of location – she loved her sports, fanatically supporting Liverpool and utterly loathing Manchester United. She was a sporty gal.

But was she really a porn star, rather than a 118 phone girl? Or was this an exceptional one-off, easy money, a wish to rebel against her parents, or (more likely) revenge against a despotic boyfriend? I doubt I'll ever find out, for she will never tell me.

It made no difference anyway. I'd had enough surprises for one day and it was time to go to sleep. I threw the magazine on the floor and got ready for bed.

Chapter 18

The fourteenth of May, AD 2001 was my first day at the Pall Mall *stroika*. My main responsibility was the building of partition walls, both stud work and plasterboard tackling. I'd become quite good at this by now.

The same day some other important things took place, for example, the whole world almost ending forever. The end of the world, by the way, began with one of Nansen's clever ideas on how to become rich. This time, it was his opium poppies business, his idiotic attempt to brew home-made heroin based on hazy recollections of old hippy tales about how to create the variety called hanka. In retrospect, it seems such an unpleasant business that anybody should find the idea of making it revolting. Anyhow, the fourteenth of May, as we were to find out, was destined to develop into a very memorable day indeed.

I don't know what happened that day in Israel, but over in London, it was just another peaceful day. In the morning, I had a cup of tea and a sandwich, then covered the still sleeping Valdas with a blanket as he looked cold and miserable, grabbed my heavy carpenter's chest and went off to support capitalism with my work and sweat.

My brain has this stupid quality that doesn't allow me to make decisions instantaneously. On only rare occasions have I managed to go through all the pros and cons very fast, so my usual tactic is to wait and give my neurons a bit of time to rearrange themselves in new patterns. I never follow the first impulse, to avoid making stupid decisions. The working day passed quickly, cutting two-by-fours and banging them together in stud walls. Meanwhile, the cogs were turning around in my brain with a squeaky noise, until by the end of the day I had made a firm decision not to call the police about what Valdas had told me. First, it was my own ass on the line as well as his, for I was there just as illegally as most of the Lithuanian chippies. Second, if I made another anonymous call, they would interrogate Moses Kwaku who, I was guessing, had also played an important role in the hiding of the corpse. And Moses could point his finger at me. Neither did I wish Moses and Celia any harm. They had countless dependent kids after all. Even though Darius Maisiulis used to be an orphan and a widower when alive, getting the police involved would not help him in any way, not to mention all his friends, who would get into trouble if interrogations started. Now, when the European Union has abolished all its internal borders, it all sounds stupid. Back then it was the cruel reality.

Another line of thought concerned the titmag. I wondered who else knew about Rahima. Admittedly, my recollections of the photos provoked me to stupid, uncontrollable grinning, and I knew the Devil would definitely try to pull my tongue next time I saw Rahima. But then, how was I to tackle it? Nice conversation starter – hey, I've seen your nude pics in a mag. Me too, she'd probably say and shrug.

Or maybe not. More likely, I'd get kicked in the nuts and/or get seriously beaten with a cast iron frying pan – there actually was one in our kitchen. She was prone to being pissed off easily, remember.

So I decided to go home and do nothing. Maybe have some cheap, weak piss like Heineken or something and watch an action film. Yet it turned out that other people had plans too, and theirs were to interfere with mine. When I arrived home, I discovered that Valdas had gone – most likely back to church. Rahima was home, though, as I could hear sexy giggles coming from her room.

Nansen appeared as soon as I got out of the shower. He had this smell of rotting leaves and smoke coming off him, and an Aldi bag filled with dirty clothes and his sleeping bag to go in our washing machine. Plus, in his rucksack, as he explained enthusiastically, he had the paint solvent, dimedrol, sodium carbonate, vinegar, the camping cooker I had given him and the enamel saucepan. Even though I was against him brewing hanka at my place – *for Christ's sake, why couldn't he do it in the woods by himself?* – I still couldn't deny an old friend use of my shower and washing machine. He had literally nothing on him that didn't smell like smoked herring, so I lent him my white Primark bathrobe and the rest went into the washing machine.

While Nansen was in the shower, I opened a can of Heineken and prepared in my mind the list of reasons why he was not allowed to make hanka in our house. At that moment, a distant singing started out on the street. It grew steadily louder until it was evidently coming from somewhere very close by. The main door opened downstairs and the singing entered the house under me, apparently reaching journey's end in our living room.

The song appeared to be about Jerusalem. 'Oh Jerusalem, Jerusalem, you new bright City of Faith.' There was a sound of furniture being moved and a child crying. It felt wrong and even scary to go downstairs now – I knew I wouldn't fit in the company. On the other hand, it was intriguing, since this was supposed to be the last day of existence.

'Praise the Lord!'

'Amen!'

Without a shadow of a doubt, it was the weird doctor again. He started the next tune, "Oh Father high in Heaven, look down upon thy sons". The loose glass in the garden door rattled as it was pushed open, and a crowd of people flowed into the garden, all looking – well, how to put it tactfully – like a mob of sectarians, really. Altogether there were some thirty people, maybe ten of them children, all dressed up in white smocks and carrying little black books. The women wore kerchiefs on their heads, while the men had bare heads. I opened the window and waved. Rimantas and both Stans waved back, and Valdas immediately came upstairs. All his desperation and indecisiveness had vanished; either because of the absolution I had granted him yesterday or for some other reason; he seemed completely transformed now. He was freshly shaven and had a natural rouge to his cheeks, his eyes glistening and his voice that of a happily uplifted parishioner.

"Hi!" I greeted him. I was trying to sound casual and offhand, and not to show any surprise at the eccentric goings-on outside. "What brings you here? I thought you weren't coming back."

Valdas looked undeniably dignified in his white karategi costume. All his being seemed to emanate deep compassion for me for not having one. He bent his head and regarded me with great seriousness.

"Willis, this is probably your last and only chance. The people downstairs have gathered here especially because I asked them to come over and help me to open your heart with the power of prayer. We were going to stay in the church, but Doctor Butt said that this is the most important day in human history, and we must offer a last chance to everyone. And so we went into the street, to preach for one last time, and I insisted we come to visit this house. I knew you would be at home! That is a good sign in itself – it means the Lord is giving you a chance! Relax, let the Holy Spirit take you in its hands."

I was being offered the possibility of avoiding extinction in a lake of fire. Logically, I couldn't lose anything by joining Valdas and his group – if they were right, I would be lifted up in the air and spared the tribulations of universal catastrophe. If, on the other hand, Doctor Butt had miscalculated, I would simply have a night out in my own garden.

Downstairs, an emotional 'ula laka moga huka nana buttarra akaoooooooh' from one of the ladies present cut through the song. 'Hallelujah!' everybody else exclaimed. 'Vula matara lala lula,' she continued, and her voice changed so she sounded rather like a dog barking at the moon, her outburst culminating in a disturbing howl. Gradually the rhythm of the song fell apart, as though the choir had lost its leader, and only a couple of voices remained to hold the melody.

Valdas looked at me expectantly. I couldn't help it – I was just too shy to surrender myself to the guidance of the Holy Spirit. I coughed. "Valdas, I guess I'm not really…"

The song had ended and now a different voice, one which I did not recognise, started to sing a new one, in English with a heavy Lithuanian accent. Valdas grabbed my hand and without listening to me started to pull me downstairs.

"Come downstairs just for a second, and hang out with us a little. It's not only about you being saved from hell, but also about your friends and flatmates. You will not refuse to say hello to Rimantas and both Stans, will you?"

Of course, I couldn't refuse to say hello. *What is there in me, this soft creature, that allows itself to be pushed around or exploited by everybody?* I let Valdas drag me downstairs. He propelled me forcibly into the middle of the crowd outside, where I found myself exchanging wary looks with Doctor Butt. I don't even know if he recognised me. If he did, it would probably only be as just another face in the sea of builders he had hired throughout his life. He had seen me only once, and that was quite a while ago. And, sad though it might sound, I have nothing noticeable or remarkable about my person.

In any case, he was more interested in singing. For a moment, the vision of a dead builder with a bloody halo around his head flashed before my eyes, but it was quickly gone. The emotions around me grew more and more intense, and more people started to speak in tongues. It felt scary and exciting at the same time. They gathered around me like a crowd of zombies, except for two boys about ten years of age who sat on the grass and loudly called out the name of Jesus. The atmosphere didn't allow for anything reasonable, such as excusing myself and leaving. People grabbed each other's hands and began to sway from one side to the other. I was trapped.

"Open your heart, Willis!" yelled Valdas somewhere behind my back.

"First close your eyes, though, it is much easier that way," advised another Lithuanian, whom I haven't seen before.

"All in your hands, oh Lord," Rimantas chanted as he swayed to and fro. He switched to English to address everybody. "Will wants to open himself to God – he has understood everything and appreciates this last chance to be saved! Let us pray to the Lord to save Will along with all true believers! It is time for the breaking of the seals![33]"

"Amen!"

It feels ungrateful to turn around and leave when some thirty people are doing their very best to drag you out of hell. And you feel distinctly stupid when they sing and talk in languages not only you but they themselves cannot understand. I didn't feel inside my own shoes, to put it mildly.

---

[33] According to the Revelation of John, the Apocalypse will start when the Lamb (i.e. Christ) breaks the seven seals on a mysterious scroll. As each seal is opened, various plagues and catastrophes will attack the Earth (Revelation, Ch.5).

Yet it became even worse when I lifted my eyes and spotted Nansen in the window of my room, hands folded on his chest, his long, wet black hair loose on the white shoulders of my Primark bathrobe. It was getting dark, but I swear I could see a big grin on his face. He was definitely getting a huge kick out of watching us.

Then things progressed rapidly from being merely stupid to becoming annoying and irksome. The circus around me continued as Rimantas took hold of one of my hands while somebody else took the other and I became a part of the magic circle. Everybody was still singing. *Didn't they ever get tired or fed up with singing the same old stuff over and over?* I looked around. No one seemed to be getting bored. The same melody continued for a long, long time, perhaps some twenty minutes before, without a pause, Doctor Butt launched us into the next one. The setting sun fell behind the Leyton skyline and outside our garden; the streets of London were lit up by rows of pearly street lamps and the yellow rectangles of residential windows. Desperately, I looked towards mine. Nansen was still standing there, but there appeared to be a weak bluish light behind his shoulder, presumably coming from a source somewhere on the floor. It was the same blue you get from the flame of a little camping stove.

'Jerusalem, Jerusaleeem!' sang a lady right next to me. She looked very English and had arrived at our end of the world party wearing little silver earrings and a thick layer of make-up. Why none of the neighbours had so far objected to the racket we were making was beyond me. But then it occurred to me that it wasn't that late really despite the fact that it was now quite dark.

The bluish light made me sigh inwardly. So Nansen hadn't listened to me. He didn't care about my warnings and all I had said; he had simply put his fucking poppies in the pot of boiling solvent and was now busy getting the liquid to evaporate.

Evaporating the solvent? Was that really what he was doing? Yes, it looked like it. But what was he doing now, the bloody imbecile (sorry, Nansen), the boneheaded nincompoop, the plain and simple idiot – and what did the suspicious movements his silhouette was making against the background of the cooker flame mean? Was I dreaming – or was he really rolling up a cigarette, sticking it in his mouth, then getting out a box of matches, shaking it to make sure in the dark that there were still some inside, then turning away from the draught, and lighting a match? Was he REALLY that stupid? Or was I just letting my imagination run away with me in the thickening darkness of a mad spring evening?

A mighty splash of light cut across the dusk. With a dampened boom my room exploded into flames that erupted through the window and shot out at us. The image of Nansen, with his Jesus-like goatee and long hair and an expression of surprise and puzzlement on his face, was imprinted on my retina. He had his arms wide open, as if he was trying to catch the flaming fireball that had just flown out through the window, then he slowly fell to one side and disappeared from view. With a sharp crack, the curtain rail detached from the wall and together with the massive, fake Victorian pelmet collapsed onto him. We froze, the singing stopped, and everybody's eyes stayed fixed on the window.

Now, at this point, it is crucial that you fully understand the technology of at-home heroin-making and the role of household appliances in this process. First, you take poppies with pods, dry them (technically, the drier they are, the easier they are to measure out and work with, though it's not that important really), then you grate a cup of poppies together with two tablespoons of sodium bicarbonate and add some hundred cubic centimetres of boiling water. I've heard that truly hardcore guys use ammonium instead, however, sodium is easier to find and doesn't stink so bad. Warm it up, add the paint solvent and leave the beverage to simmer for some ten minutes. Opium alkaloids become separated from the stems and enter the liquid. Everything turns brownish-green (hence its name 'zelyonka', or 'the green') and stinks like hell. Take a rag, philtre the green soup through it. Then, it goes back on the heat again. Simmer, until there is only a little cloudy mud at the very bottom; it will harden in a few minutes. Dilute and boil it up again. Meanwhile, the vapour spreads everywhere and stinks like the worst of Beelzebub's typhoidal discharges; it is worth to keep in mind that it is also highly combustible, so watch out at this stage for open flames and sparks. Now, add some vinegar and allow the chemistry to work. When the residue has settled on the bottom you philtre it once more, boil the liquid out one more time and, for the last time, add some water. Add ground Diphenhydramine. Stir well. You're ready to serve.

Almost, that is.

An important notice: if you will make heroin according to this recipe, you're going to fail. A couple of ingredients are missing. I don't want to pretend to be highly moral or anything, for any person who has the dedication to exterminate himself or herself will surely manage to do so even without my guidance, yet I refuse to give the full recipe of this Devil's brew. To understand my story, you only need to know the basics, so here they are, and that's all. As to the rest, my lips are zipped and my keyboard shut.

As you can, I'm sure, gather so far, the most critical is the first round of evaporation, when the solvent is in the air. This makes it, as we all know, a highly flammable substance. Over these years my anger at Nansen has practically gone and I have become able to see the funny side of the story. And now, when I close my eyes, I can still see before me the little camping stove, thrusting with a silent hiss blue flames under a dirty enamel saucepan. 'Shshshshshsss' hums the stove; 'gurgurgurgle' purrs the liquid in the pan; 'chirp!' goes the match as it lights in Nansen's hand; and then 'BOOM!' goes the whole damn room.

The explosion, quite understandably, gripped everybody's undivided attention.

'*Vardan Dievo Tevo*[34].' one of the women gasped as she plucked a child up in her arms.

Mind you, even I had an apocalyptic feeling by now.

'*Jezau!*[35]' yelled Rimantas.

He and another geezer dashed into the house as swift as a couple of antelopes. I hurried after them. I wanted to be in there first, to hide those idiotic poppies. I won't deny that kicking Nansen in the nuts also was a tempting part of the plan.

The others got to my room first, however. One of them opened the door, looked around, then stepped back.

"Must be the wrong room. There's no one here," he said in Russian.

---

[34] In the name of God the Father. *(Lithuanian)*

[35] Jesus!(Lithuanian)

Behind me, I could hear the growing murmur of voices and the stomping of feet as the rest of the congregation gathered up the courage to follow us.

"No, it is," Rimantas insisted. After all, he had been living in this house for quite a while and he wasn't so easily confused by the layout of its room. As he was standing behind the two others on the narrow staircase, he tried to push himself through, causing one of the others to stumble back and accidently – unless it was Providence intervening – pushed open the door to Rahima's room.

The yellowish light from the twenty-five watt corridor bulb spilt into the darkened room and we all automatically looked that way.

To say that we were stunned would be an underestimation.

It is probably worth reminding you, dear reader, that one of Rahima's guy friends was called Clemente – the one with round spectacles, long hair, and the dream of starting his own internet business. Nice chap, intelligent, quiet, yet pleasantly sociable. However, still waters run deep, as they say. I might have mentioned before that it was Clemente who was able to get the longest recitals of rhythmic 'Oh my Gods' out of Rahima. And at this moment, right there, it was him we marvelled at – although initially we didn't know it was him.

In the dusk of Rahima's crimson painted room (she adored the colour as the tone of passion, aggression and sex) stood two people dressed in something rubbery and rather shapeless, which made it difficult to guess the sex of the wearer. Their costumes presented red, black and creamy overtones. In various places, latex exposed bits of living, accessible flesh. One of the figures held in its hand – no, not a whip – a cleaning duster in the colours of the rainbow. The other figure, who on closer examination, appeared to be female, wore something resembling a scuba diver's corselet.

The window had a blind over it and the tall candles they had placed on the floor threw yellow reflections on the surface of the latex. Two heads in shiny balaclavas swivelled towards us, one scarlet, the other creamy, but they didn't say a word. The one who was probably a man raised the duster as if in self-defence, while the one who was probably a woman placed her hands belligerently on her hips. They must have been surprised no less than we were, with the explosion and all that. And now a white-clad sect breaking into their love nest.

Everyone froze.

"WHATTA FUCKING FUCK YOU FUCKING WANT? WHY DOES EVERYONE HAVE TO FUCKING PISS ME OFF ALL THE FUCKING TIME?"

I was right. It was her.

Chapter 19

Subsequent events unfolded in a dynamic fashion. The staircase and hall had filled up with people wearing white karategis. Those at the back were bumping into those at the front, stretching their necks to see better and whispering amongst themselves. You could bet the explosion would have attracted the attention of the neighbours, especially after the orgies of chanting and glossolalia they had already been treated to. I cast a look at their worried faces, but in my own head, there were completely different thoughts.

The house stank of boiled solvent, especially my room— "Can you feel the brimstone?" someone enquired in a quiet voice downstairs. Somehow, I had to get rid of any evidence of our activity—solvent, burner, poppies, dimedrol and possibly handicapped Nansen…AND NANSEN!

All this ran through my brain at the speed of light, but in the same instant that I got it, both latex lovers came straight at us.

"How dare you!" ejaculated the cream mask in English, with a strong South American accent. "We're not disturbing anyone!"

"*I'm* gonna disturb *them*!" yelled the crimson mask in Rahima's voice.

With the duster raised high, they advanced on us.

At this moment, Rimantas did something no one expected, although admittedly there was a certain logic to it under the circumstances. He fell to his knees in front of the kinky latex couple, struck his forehead against the floor and started to howl a prayer. Oh Lord, Thy will be done, save the damned, etcetera, etcetera. His body was right on the threshold, blocking the door. Rahima was startled, to say the least. First, she must have been utterly at a loss to know why a group of men in white karate robes had come rushing into her room at a most intimate moment, and second, she must have been more than a little surprised when one of them evidently began to worship her in front of all the others.

Meanwhile, the rest of the congregation downstairs had no bloody clue what was going on upstairs and only had the expressions on our faces to go by. Not surprisingly, they quickly figured that something damn special must be going on upstairs to make us all look like we did—and the sight of one of their most respected community members kneeling and praying in front of something they couldn't see must have confirmed it for them. One after another, they fell to their knees and started praying too.

It was now or never, so I took advantage of the madness of the moment to slip into my room, closing the door behind me.

The reason the Lithuanians hadn't spotted Nansen was that he had fallen behind the bed, where he had been covered from top to toe by the set of curtains and the massive Victorian pelmet. The thick material of the old curtains must have stifled the flames before they could set fire to the whole house. The stench was incredible; paint solvents possess very powerful olfactory properties and the evaporating procedure makes them even worse.

As soon as I had closed the door, a shapeless heap of dusty curtain slowly emerged from behind the bed. It was Nansen, looking like he was playing a shrouded ghost for Halloween. With a low moan, he pulled the yellow and green curtain off his head.

"Sorry, man, that was really stupid!" he yelled at me. I realised the bang had deafened him for a spell.

There was too much anger in me to risk a reply. What worried me more were the stars of excitement in Nansen's eyes, which made him look even more like a true madman, perfectly capable of further insanities.

"Where are the poppies and all the other stuff?" I asked after a second or two, speaking loudly than I cared to so that he could hear me.

"Er..." Nansen helplessly drew a wide circle that took in the whole space around us.

Understood. The shit could be anywhere in the room.

"If the cops come," I hissed at him, "you tell them you spilt the solvent by accident, and it exploded because you were smoking in the room, got it? We kept the solvent because we were going to paint the door, got it?"

Not a brilliant solution, but still better than nothing. It was the first thing that came to mind, and the main objective was for both of us to come up with the same story when interrogated separately.

Luckily the newspapers with the few remaining dry poppies were right beside the bed. I wrapped everything up in my blanket—it was all stained with *zelyonka* anyway, ergo unwashable—including the stove, the enamel saucepan, and most of the greenish witch's brew that I was able to scrape off the carpet. The titmag, still rolled up into a glossy tube, had also fallen on the floor. I tossed it on the bed, grabbed the bulging blanket and rushed out of the room, thinking about the rubbish bins on a parallel street to ours. At the rate things were developing, it seemed the only feasible course to take.

However, time moves at different speeds in different universes, even if they are parallel. While I was dealing with the evidence of our crime in the bedroom, apocalyptic passions were brewing on the landing just outside my door. When I opened it, I found landing and stairs still full of Butt's flock, while Rahima was still in her room, with Rimantas crouching on the floor. Clemente had positioned himself right behind his woman, and was still waving his duster, pathetically.

"I'm not destroying anybody's fucking party, SO FUCK OFF! IDIOTS!"

"Yes!" screeched Clemente behind her. "Not good neighbours! You're just impolite people!"

Meanwhile, for the true believers, the party really seemed to be getting started. In retreat from the latex demons above, many of them withdrew to the living room, where they busied themselves speaking in tongues, kneeling and rhythmically rocking backwards and forwards. They prayed in languages that definitely sounded distinctive to each performer, so it was a case of glossolalia again, not xenolalia, I supposed. Nobody really paid any attention to me or the blanket wrapped up in my hands, so I summoned up my courage and started descending towards the exit.

As I reached the lowest step, someone shouted upstairs, and I looked back up. Rahima had proceeded from words to action.

She had bent down, grabbed Rimantas by his shoulders, and was now trying to push him off her threshold. Clemente hastened to help, and they managed to lift him, still in his embryonic position, and to lay him in the middle of the landing. The sight of two rubber-wrapped creatures, quite likely the Devil's own spawn, carrying one of their fellow-believers caused predictable unrest among the others still on the stairs. This seemed to make the spawn themselves even angrier, and the one in the red mask shook a crimson fist towards the crowded stairs and the living room below.

"BASTARDS! WHY DON'T YOU ALL GO TO HELL AND LEAVE US ALONE!"

"Apanaktara, shoolwahooyallayalla," responded Rimantas from the floor, and then suddenly in one sweeping motion, was back on square one—Rahima's threshold. "Aramatara, crinkycroogiekranx!" he cried as he hit the floor with his forehead in praise of the Lord.

The red demon was momentarily lost for words and started to grapple with Rimantas once more, grabbing him by the hips and pulling him back to the landing, then, with a loud squeak from her costume, pushed him downstairs, where he was received into the caring arms of his brethren.

"Pumpkin, isn't that a bit harsh?" the demon in the creamy mask suddenly enquired.

The demon in the scarlet mask rounded on him.

"Shut up, you bloody wimp!" she hissed. "If you can't fuck a woman, then at least you could have thrown these idiots out of the room! Oh, pumpkin," she went on, her voice acquiring a mocking Spanish accent. "I seem to have a little problem here— I need an inspirational boost of some kind! Go fuck yourself, Mister Limp Rubberdick! I don't want to see you again! Ever!"

With that she thrust the stunned Nicaraguan away from her and darted back into her room, slamming the door.

"Rahima! My bunnybaby!" exclaimed poor Clemente as he gripped the door handle.

Regrettably, bunnybaby wasn't in the mood anymore. Rahima opened a narrow slit in the door just enough to get her red lips, framed by even redder latex, right in the crack.

"Fuck off! Don't come around when your cock isn't working, got it? You are fucking PISSING ME OFF, don't you fucking understand?"

Her door slammed again and we could hear the sound of furniture being dragged across the floor—she was so PISSED OFF that she was barricading herself in her room.

"Bitch!" the Nicaraguan spat through clenched teeth. Then suddenly conscious of the many eyes looking at him, he slowly pulled the mask off his face and plodded heavily down the stairs, scowling as he yelled back at her over his shoulder. "You'll remember this!"

Upstairs, something solid hit the door from the inside. *That was Rahima's desk*, I thought. *No one will shift that in a hurry.*

Clemente reached the lowest step where I stood with my blanket full of stuff, and raised his eyes to the ceiling. "Oh God, please help me to punish this woman!"

It was the most heartfelt prayer I'd heard all day.

I must point out, just in case you're wondering, that all this happened at incredible speed—much faster than I can lay things down on paper. I pressed my blanket full of incriminating evidence against my chest and was about to precede Clemente towards the front door when Providence decided to stick its oar in again.

"Be careful what you wish for," spoke a voice behind me.

I looked back. It was Doctor Butt. Almost as pale as his white outfit, he stood among the shocked parishioners, glaring at Clemente with the stance of an exemplary warrior of Christ.

"The Lord might listen to you and punish her, as you wish," he continued. "But today is the final day—the Lamb is finally breaking the seals, and your words can—"

He broke off abruptly as the door to my bedroom crashed open—and there he was, stage above left, the divine Nansen. He was dressed in a white bathrobe, with his long black hair spread over his shoulders, sandals on his bare feet (yes, sandals, I'm not making this up), his beard parted in a smug smile, and a glossy, rolled up titmag in one of his hands. He stepped across the landing and then headed down towards the ground floor, carefully stepping between startled true believers.

Nansen locked eyes with me, the crack of a smile in his beard growing wider, and he raised the rolled up titmag high in the air.

'God Almighty,' somebody breathed behind my back, 'he's going to break the seals *right now*!'

Nobly and coolly, now the centre of everybody's attention, Nansen paused in his descent right above me and Clemente. The whole place fell silent and everyone stared, anxious not to miss anything important. He slowly unrolled the glossy scroll in his hand and then, with a theatrical gesture, opened up before me the two-page centrefold. Magnolia's Flower XXX stood in all her glory spread across the glossy pages, her plump lips nibbling sensually at her own manicured pinky.

"Look!" Nansen yelled at me. Obviously, he was still deaf after the explosion and all the hullaballoo of the events behind the closed door had escaped him completely. "Isn't this the girl who shares with you?"

Clemente reacted immediately.

"Biiiitch!" he yelped and seized the mag out of Nansen's hand. "You were so right about wishing," he groaned, his voice thick with emotion. With shaking hands he quickly turned page after page. "But now I know!" He looked up at us, a strange light in his eyes. "God Almighty sometimes does listen! Thank you! Thanks to the Lord! And have a good evening."

After this bewildering change in attitude, he turned his latex-clad back on us all and promptly left the building, causing an audible reaction from everybody on the way out, as there was a cut-out below the waist, right where the buttocks are.

"What did he say?" Yelled Nansen, jerking a thumb at the retreating figure. "I couldn't read his lips. Probably that damn accent of his."

Without answering I hastened outside to find somewhere to dump my rubbish.

Chapter 20

Upon my return I found angry neighbours crowding at our door, demanding peace and order. Just a little bit later, we had the full monty – ambulance, police, fire brigade and even fucking gas emergency team. The whole house got closed off with black and yellow tape. We were all herded into the street because, they said, if there had been one explosion, there might be another. For a short while, the whole bloody street was closed. Onlookers popped out of nearby houses and, in no time at all, there was an enthusiastic TV crew right there, busy filming. For a moment, we were the centre of the news universe, a feeling we didn't get to enjoy fully as we were abruptly transferred to police vans, with our faces covered so that no one would recognise us on TV (*what was that for*, I wonder?).

What shall I tell you about the British prison system? My impression was that the cells look just like the ones in gangster films everybody has seen, with painted brickwork and bunk beds. Even the interrogation room had the iconic one-sided mirror. And there were detectives slurping tea with milk during the interrogation, though I was never offered one.

I felt more than a little surprised when they released me the very next day after I had signed a paper saying that I would not leave London any time soon. The explosion episode was apparently being put down to an accident with paint solvent (we're builders, after all, and we'd admitted Nansen smoked in bed – ha, ha). As for the presence of the true believers, I simply told the truth: most of them were my flatmates, who just happened to be awaiting the end of the world in our garden. The detectives kept their poker faces on, so I never found out what they really thought of that. The end of the world scenario, however, explained everything. Like, absolutely everything.

As we left, we were met by some folk from the Latvian embassy, who asked us a number of questions the British hadn't thought of asking, such as, are you working here, do you have enough money to live on, and so on. It was something we had never expected from our own kind, especially after the local police hadn't bothered with such things. All in all, the whole sorry saga really damaged my nervous system. For a while, I was convinced that Nansen and I would get thrown into prison for years, or simply sent back home, yet the cops were surprisingly tolerant. Most likely they understood quite clearly that we were illegal, but they didn't make too much fuss about it. It felt like we were running on a knife edge, if you know what I mean. Altogether, the whole process was a nightmare of such proportions it deserves a separate book, really. If readers of this book behave – by which I mean buy lots of copies – I'll have to write a sequel with a title like *The Trial* or *Stroika-2*. Anyhow, keeping the juridical stuff aside for possible future publication allows me to hurry on and share the most diverting info about how my story ends.

Among the most important consequences of our 'accident' was the fact that Doctor Butt ended up in prison. Apparently his end-of-world activities lead someone to believe it might be a good idea to give his church a closer inspection. Most of the true believers worked for his company and there proved to be some issues with taxes. I personally don't think any of his workers ever paid the Queen a single penny. The second issue was, as you might have guessed, Health and Safety. Valdas eventually gave up and told the cops all about the manslaughter. This added more grave charges: manslaughter and concealing evidence of it from the authorities. Interestingly, Moses was never mentioned; in fact, Butt took all the blame and claimed he hid the evidence himself. Whether he did it because the angels told him to, I don't know, but in any case, it also saved my ass, and I do feel grateful for that. As for me as a witness, I can say with relief that since nobody has ever asked, I have never said anything.

Butt's followers, on the other hand, believe that he's in prison because it is all part of God's plan, whereby Butt is commissioned to save the souls of inmates while amongst them. Be that as it may, a couple of years behind the bars and our doctor has started an internet blog, on which he reports weekly on his progress. According to the blog, so far he has managed to convert twelve people. Hallelujah!

Soon after the end of the world was over, Nansen borrowed money from someone and left Europe, apparently forever, and is now settled in India. All the best, mate! Send us a postcard once in a while, OK?

A most interesting story has developed around Rahima. The end of the world, as one might have expected, had her very much pissed off, so she left our house without any goodbyes but also with a month's worth in unpaid rent, gas, and electricity, never mind the council tax. However, karma works in mysterious ways. Recently somebody forwarded me an internet link to a website called *www.saintrahima.com,* which is devoted to none other than her good self. Admittedly, it looks like Rahima has nothing to do with it and the chances are she doesn't know anything about it. Something tells me it could be the revenge of a once latex-clad IT specialist.

The website describes the end of the world as we encountered it. Yes! The end of the world, so it says, was scheduled for the fourteenth of May 2001, and the eye of the hurricane, as it were, happened to be in Leyton, East London. The rain of fire and brimstone began, the trumpets sounded as thunder, and Jesus himself descended in a cloud of flame. He even started breaking the seals on the mystery scroll. Then, however, he disappeared, and that is because Saint Rahima prayed for mankind with such devotion, offering herself to the Lord as a 'pure nugget of human chastity and virtue' in order to pay for the sins of humankind once again. 'For not one of those who have been born mortal have ever been so innocent and far from the sin as Saint Rahima.' claims the website under the 'Biography' section. The website also offers T-shirts carrying the logo of the saint and a series of books called 'Conversations with St Rahima'.

And that's how the world was saved on 14/05/2001.

How do I know it really is about our gal? Why, they have her photos there. The site features my favourite photo from the titmag, the one where she exercises on a treadmill. The lower part of the image is cut off, and around her beautiful face there is an oval frame with rays of light emanating from it. The serious yet devoted facial expression she has in that photo really makes her look like a saint. If you click on the tab 'Friends', you can find a link to Butt's prison blog and a short biography. It turns out he has a PhD in English. The website also contains – and this is truly impressive – some recipes for the Lent period, as well as for immediately after Lent. In the 'after' section, there is a vegetable stew with stuffed pork fillets, called 'Rahimka', a recipe uploaded by a fan from Lithuania. Pork. How ironic.

The only person I'm in regular contact with after all these years, is Valdas. He also had to go to court. They dropped the charge of manslaughter against him but put him in prison for concealing information from the police, as well as for working illegally in the UK. He did his sentence in Lithuania and has sent me a few e-mails from there. He hasn't mentioned God in any of them. It will be interesting to meet him and have a chat if he returns to the London *stroika* again. After all, citizens of the Baltic states don't need business visas to work in England anymore.

As for myself, I have enrolled at a university to study architecture. If the building game is to be my fate, then I prefer to go for less work and more money. I live in East London with my new girlfriend, who is a Kiwi and also happens to be a classmate, and we are trying to do some windsurfing in our spare time. I don't know how much surfing time there will be available to us, though, as the mom of my kids is moving to London too. Through some friends, she has found a job in a pub in Kensington. The main thing is that my new girlfriend is cool with me having kids from a previous relationship, and that's one of the reasons why I love and treasure her so much!

Epilogue

In conclusion – some thoughts of a builder. All those years ago, when the economic misery of my motherland forced me onto a path of thorns leading to London, people like me were few and far between. It was scary to leave home. Now the very concept of home has changed. The world has shrunk. Very few people these days haven't travelled the world or tried working elsewhere than their place of birth.

I guess mine is a story about culture shock. No, about two shocks. The first strikes you when you arrive in your new place of residence, and the second when you return home. It's a scary experience, seeing your old self from the outside, in the faces of those you left behind.

Now, don't get the wrong idea and think that all immigrants are incompetent butterfingers. There are loads of brilliant carpenters, virtuoso plumbers, gifted turners and excellent scaffolders. However, the simple logic of immigration dictates that such people almost never become pioneers. If you are good at a trade, you are normally quite busy and can earn enough where you already are. And if you are well off financially, why should you take the trouble to immigrate? In a way, we first immigrants were unable to start a good life where we were born, so we went to discover and conquer the outside world. But what a survival school it had been! If Latvia was a bottle of champagne and life the bottle shaker, it was my destiny to be the cork sent flying who knows where. My motherland didn't have enough milk for all her children, and I was nudged away from her breasts by more successful individuals. I went for the next survival strategy available.

Just as I'm writing this, I have taken on a private job with a couple of my mates. It's the refurbishment of a lovely Georgian house in Richmond. The first thing we discovered on our first day working together was that if we were to establish a company, the most appropriate name for it would be 'The Three Bachelors', even though we are all married or have girlfriends. Why? Because the house is being roofed, plastered, plumbed up, bricked up, fixed, painted and refurbished by a Bachelor of History, a Bachelor of Economics and a Bachelor of Anthropology. The only useful aspect of our higher education from top Eastern European universities, it has turned out, was a tangential exposure to English.

What consequences will current immigration have in the future? From the perspective of the colonists – i.e. those who venture into new strange lands full of resources to till the soil, toil at the till and then send the hard-earned profits back home, in other words, from the perspective of the immigrants – immigration leads to what I consider *true globalisation*. It is like marvelling at the world via YouTube and wanting to change your life because of what you see. Cultural and mental changes that come from the inside and are not imposed by outsiders. Many immigrant colonists in the UK have ended up going native, simply because they find British values more reasonable. And they decide to stay.

Which leads to the next issue: their kids will grow up essentially British. And as Britons, they won't be happy with the lifestyle their émigré parents were happy with when younger. Labouring on a *stroika*? Kitchen portering? Road sweeping? No, thanks, we're British. The wealthy countries offer the promise of a good life, but if you end up sharing a house with ten other people, working twelve-hour shifts, and still being paid the minimum wage, the promise turns out to be broken. And the whole bloody cycle will start again…

I have seen religious devotion. I don't buy it. I've seen hard work. It hasn't made me rich. It is being a human being among human beings that has given me everything worth having.

The builder has spoken.